GIRL with a Fly Rod

Fly fishing For Young Women

RIVER GIRLS REV 2ND ED

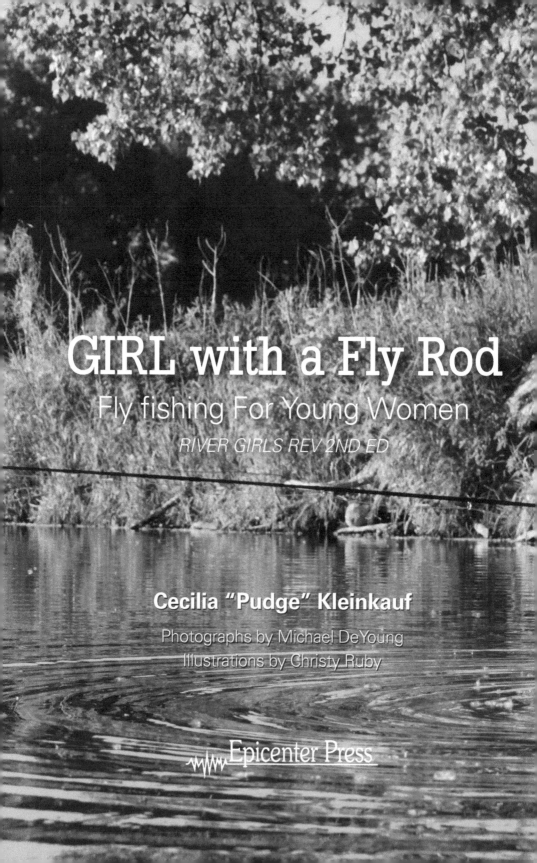

GIRL with a Fly Rod

Fly fishing For Young Women

RIVER GIRLS REV 2ND ED

Cecilia "Pudge" Kleinkauf

Photographs by Michael DeYoung
Illustrations by Christy Ruby

Epicenter Press

Cover design Dawn Anderson
Front cover photo courtesy of: Mattias P. Rosell
Back cover photo courtesy of: Chris J. Korich
Interior design Rudy Ramos

ISBN 9781941890530

The 2nd Edition of the River Girls book is dedicated to

Lou Anne Dowling,

editor of the original River Girls book.

Lou Anne passed away early in 2018. She was with me from my very first book, inspiring me to carry on the work of leading women and girls to take up the sport I love through book after book. I have a very large place in my heart where Lou Ann still resides and always will.

May She Rest in Peace

Table of Contents

Foreword

I first met Pudge Kleinkauf in 1996, during the International Women's Fly Fishing (IWFF) Festival in Baja, Mexico. At that time, I couldn't believe there were so many other women participating in my favorite sport, fly fishing! I felt fortunate to have met those fly fishing women, and they have become a wonderful support system for me in my fly fishing endeavors and in my life.

For twenty years or more, Pudge has encouraged women to try out the sport of fly fishing through her business, Women's Fly fishing. She's taught scores of women to fly fish and introduced them to the incredible freshwater fishing opportunities in Alaska. Her first book, Fly Fishing Women Explore Alaska, has done much to demonstrate that this is a perfect sport for women. Now, River Girls will do the same for girls.

At that same festival in Mexico, I met Alyssa, one of the river girls featured in this book. What a treat it was to see her down on the beach, fishing right along with all the adult women! I also know Seline, one of the adult women who relates her life as a fly fisher in River Girls.

Even though I don't know all the girls and women featured in this book, I certainly know other river girls who are much like Alyssa, Samantha, Alex, and Blair. And thanks to organizations such as the! WFF, I've met many, many women like Seline, Ellie, BethAnn, and Ann, the river women of this book.

Fly fishing is about the beauty of nature, but much of the pleasure of it for me comes from sharing good sportsmanship, creating memories with new friends I've made while fishing, and the fun of just telling fishing stories. You will always find friendship in fly fishing wherever you go, sharing your experiences and your stories.

You'll also find that this wonderful sport will be with you through good times and bad. I'm a good example of that. I am deaf.

As I lost my hearing and endured four surgeries for cochlear implants to be able to hear again, my love of fly fishing and the support of friends I'd made in the sport, like those in the WFF, helped tremendously to see me through. Those women were so accepting of my hearing disability. It's still hard for me to believe that I was elected the first president of this wonderful group of women in 1997.

You just don't know all the ways fly fishing will affect your life.

I started fly fishing in 1989 and was fortunate enough to get to travel to twenty countries to fly fish, including Costa Rica, Argentina, Australia, Senegal, Morocco, Seychelles, South Africa, and Canada. In 1996, I caught my first world-record fish in Morocco. It was a white marlin weighing in at 82.5 pounds, the largest fish of that kind ever caught on a fly rod at that time.

In those days, the International Game Fish Association (IGFA), the keepers of world records, didn't have a separate category for women's fly-rod records. Our fish had to compete with those caught by men, who had been setting records for over thirty years. After years of trying to catch a world record, it dawned on me that it was time for a change in that system and that it was up to me to make it happen. Well, it took three years of effort by lots of people and an extensive letter-writing campaign, but finally the IGFA Board of Directors established a fly-rod, world-record category for women in 1997. Hooray!

Since then, it has been amazing to see how quickly the records have come in. Over the years, I have done my best to encourage other fly fishing women to go out and seek those world-record fish. I've been very fortunate to rack up seventeen of them myself for white marlin, black marlin, Atlantic sailfish, Pacific sailfish, bonefish, bigeye trevally, dolphinfish, tarpon, and bluefin trevally. In 1998 I was named the IGFA "Angler of the Year" for setting twelve fly-rod world records in a single year, something no other woman had done.

While I'm proud of that honor, one of my greatest joys has been seeing lots of women set IGFA fly-rod world records each year. I don't want you to think that fly fishing is all about records-far from it-but it was one place I could contribute to the sport and to the women who love it.

I hope one day to meet and know many _of you who take up fly fishing with the help of River Girls. Alyssa and the other river girls are just a few of the many young women taking up fly fishing these days. Like them, you and other readers of this book will make your own contributions to the sport, just as you'll find fly fishing contributes to your life. Perhaps you'll help to spread the word to other girls about this wonderful way to be outdoors. Maybe it will be you who continues to encourage the fly fishing industry to adapt equipment to the needs of girls and women and to offer more gear for young people. Youth fly fishing classes are popping up all over, and it might be you who starts one in your own community just a few years from now.

Like Pudge, I want to encourage all girls to try the sport of fly fishing! Take advantage of the opportunity this book provides-along with the help of a parent, a relative, an instructor, or a friend-to learn a great outdoor activity. It's time you got started.

May fly fishing bring to you as much joy as it has brought to me.

Jodie Pate

Preface

It was 2006 when an out-of-the-ordinary fly-fishing book appeared on the horizon. The book highlighted four young women learning how to fish with a fly rod. Young people of either gender (especially girls) were scarce in the industry at that time, and it didn't receive much attention. But the Benjamin Franklin Book Awards, the most renowned book competition in the country, held each year by the Publishers Marketing Association, did pay attention, and awarded it the first-place Gold award in the Sports and Outdoor Recreation Competition in 2007.

Here is part of the press release from the publisher.

New York, May 31, 2007—Big Earth Publishing is proud to announce that Cecilia "Pudge" Kleinkauf has received the prestigious Benjamin Franklin Sports/Recreation Book of the Year Award for her groundbreaking new book *River Girls: Fly fishing for Young Women.*

The Benjamin Franklin Award, named in honor of America's most cherished printer and publisher, recognizes excellence in independent publishing. Publications, grouped by genre, are judged for design and editorial merit by top practitioners in each field.

In **River Girls,** the first fly fishing book ever geared toward teaching young women the sport, Kleinkauf uses the real-life experiences of four young women to create an informative and engaging introduction for pre-teen and teenage girls.

Covering everything from casting to choosing flies, Kleinkauf conveys the idea that fly fishing is not only more challenging than other types of fishing, it's more fun, too. And, it is definitely not just a sport for boys.

"This book should rival Curtis Creek Manifesto as the ideal «beginners» book. I would recommend it to anyone, regardless of sex." -Leland Miyawaki, Fishing Manager of the Orvis Store, Bellevue, WA.

Now, a young California girl, Maxine McCormick, has appeared on the horizon and is blowing the socks off the fly-fishing industry and the rest of the world. They find it hard to ignore her as she wins trophy after trophy for her fly-casting capability, which has resulted in being crowned the youngest Gold Medal casting winner of all time! Now just fourteen years old, and the winner of two gold medals at the International Fly Casting Competitions in England she has been crowned "America's Casting Princess" by an international editorial and "The Mozart of Fly-Casting" by the New York Times."

A fly caster since she was 9, while fishing with her dad she moved up to practicing casting at the famous Angler's Lodge in Golden Gate State Park in San Francisco and from there worked her way to the competitive level. The rest is history.

As the author of the River Girls book, I see Maxine as a true role model for girls and for the world of fly fishing as well. Epicenter Press is now producing a 2nd Edition of that book with the first chapter featuring Maxine so that we can show the world that there are women, young and not-so-young, that have found fly fishing to be a sport for them.

In the book Maxine describes her feelings and aspirations as she is growing up, in the fly-fishing world, and also describes her fly-fishing successes. From national fly-casting competitions to the international stage's Gold Medal she has become a peer who "talks" to young girls telling them why she likes fly-fishing and fly casting so much as well as about other sports or activities that she is participating into in high school. We certainly see her as a well-rounded girl.

Not many girls or women are likely to take up competitive fly-casting in Maxine's shadow, but they will certainly see her as a champion that shines in the fly-fishing world.

Acknowledgments

Time goes by quickly and people come in and out of our lives, and that has certainly been true about mine. During the last twelve years, the four original River Girls have grown into women with families and careers, Mike De Young has become a renowned photographer with his wife, Lori, always at his side, and was very helpful re-connecting me with the original River Girls for information about what their lives are like now. (That information is available at the end of the new book.)

Lisa Maloney, our capable editor, was "jennie" on the spot, always ready to look at the manuscript whenever I needed her, in spite of several other obligations, and a trip or two.

Lou Ann Dowling, the editor of the original book, has been with us in spirit, and Christy Ruby, our illustrator, has continued her business using Alaska animals in unique ways for her artistry. (See https://sealhuntress.wordpress.com/2017/10/)

The new book has benefited from, Phil Garrett, of Epicenter Press and Lael Morgan, the acquisitions editor (who has recently retired), who have a shared interest in a 2nd Edition. During its development Aubrey White headed up much of the actual construction, and did it smoothly.

Although not involved in the actual creation, I must thank Chris Korich, Maxine's coach, who provided ongoing insight into the day-to-day activities that Maxine was going through to help me "see" her life as she deals with the up's & down's of growing up in the midst of her life in the spotlight. From showing me the ins and outs of competitive fly fishing, with which I was only slightly familiar, to see what it might be like for Maxine to actually be "front & center," Chris, opened my eyes to a different part of the sport of fly fishing. I can't thank him enough!

Maxine is also very quick to say that her mom and dad are "behind me in every decision I make." Thanks Glenn and Simone!

The magic awaits you.

Introduction
Magic from a Wand

Once upon a time, a very lucky girl went out to the rivers with a special magic wand in her hand. The wand was a gift from a generous river woman, who had explained how to wield it. The woman said that if the girl used the wand wisely and often, it would bring her great joy.

Each time the girl visited a river with her wand, she enjoyed new smells and sounds and found new ways to pass an afternoon in blissful solitude. She discovered the beauty of streamside plants, vibrant birds, and small creatures coming to drink. Most of all, the girl learned about the mysteries of the world beneath the water. She learned that the wand could connect her to another creature living in that world, a creature very, very different from herself.

The creature was a waterling, not an earthling as she was. Instead of walking upright through the clean country air as she did, it moved without legs and rested belly down under the aqua ripples. It breathed underwater.

The girl tried to coax the waterling to come to her in the way the river woman had described. Sometimes she was successful and sometimes not. The waterling would often dart away as soon as the girl moved or, worse, just ignore her and her offerings. Still, each time the girl tried, there was excitement in seeing if she could use the wand and its magic in just the way the waterling preferred.

Recalling the river woman's wise counsel for patience, the girl would try and try again in different ways and with different enticements. Once in a while the waterling would accept her offering and let her bring him to her. Then, for a single bright moment, she would experience the wonder of his eyes watching her, the feel of his slick sides, and the living heart of a creature from another world.

Each time she was successful, she remembered the woman's advice to use the wand with wisdom and judgment. The waterling could not live in her world nor she in his. As she'd gently send him home, the girl learned about life, about beauty, about nature, and about herself.

The girl grew into womanhood with the magic wand always nearby. The nature of the magic changed and deepened as time passed, but it never disappeared. Even as she became a river woman, she was, forever and always, a river girl.

Perhaps you would like to get to know this girl. Perhaps she is you.

To find out, come along with us as some real river girls tell you about the very special world of fishing with a fly rod. You'll learn how to become a river girl, how to select and wield your own wand, where to use it, what enticements to tie onto the end of the line, and much more. Soon you will know how to connect to the waterlings in your part of the world.

The magic awaits you.

How to Use This Book

River girls are girls who fly fish. In this book you'll meet four girls who love the sport and want to share it with you. They will tell you why they think fly fishing is so special and why they recommend it. Reading their stories will give you a chance to learn more about fly fishing and why it's so appealing. Then you'll be ready to enjoy the same excitement they have found in this glorious sport.

River Girls will also help you learn the art of fly fishing. It's a book you can use in several ways, depending on how, when, and where you're getting started. Maybe you're in a fly fishing class. Maybe someone in your family is teaching you, or maybe you're learning at camp. This book can be part of your preparation. You may choose to read it all at once, or you may find certain chapters that seem especially helpful or interesting. Think of River Girls as a handbook. When you take a fly fishing class or while your folks are teaching you, this book can help you learn. When you're ready to cast a fly rod, you can refer to the sections about casting. Then you can use the advice we include about flies to help you understand which flies are used in the kinds of places where you'll be fishing. When you practice tying those flies on your line, you can get some guidance from the knots chapter, and so forth. The book also tells a little about fly fishing as a sport and how it differs from the other types of fishing.

Beyond that, River Girls includes general suggestions for lake fishing, river fishing, surf fishing, and ocean fishing to help guide you in any type of fly fishing you might try. You'll find lots of tips in these pages. We show you different flies used in different places. We explain the choices you have in fly fishing equipment. And we give suggestions for locating fishing resources in your area.

You can also use River Girls as a buying guide when you set out to acquire your own equipment. Our recommendations about the right fly rod, reel, and line for the fishing you'll be doing will help you "shop smart" (or "hint smart" about gift possibilities). The same is true for what you'll need to know about waders, boots, vests, and even underwear!

River girls are girls who flyfish.

We expect you'll read certain sections of this book at different times, as you learn to fly fish. We also think that you'll find yourself coming back to read some parts again, as you practice and gain experience. If your copy of River Girls ends up with wrinkled pages, dog-eared corners, and maybe even a few fish scales tucked away here and there, we'll have met our goal.

The river girls and I want to start you off with success on your journey as a fly fisher.

We're hoping you'll become a river girl, too.

PART ONE
Fly fishing
AND THE
River Girls

Chapter 1

Magic From A Wand, The Girl With A Flyrod

Although there were women fishing in saltwater, bass ponds, and lots of rivers before the turn of the century, it was a rare woman like Maine's "Fly Rod" Crosby," that became famous by doing it with a fly rod. Little was known about most of these women until author, Lyla Foggia, wrote her ground-breaking book, "Reel Women: The World of Women Who Fish" in 1995.

When I took up the sport in the early 1980s the fly-fishing world was still paying little, if any, attention to women and less yet to one who wanted to fly-fish in a remote unknown like Alaska. It was at a river where I was fly -fishing that women began to approach me asking me to teach them. I obliged and began to offer fly-casting lessons.

After the inception of my guiding business a couple of years later, at the urging of my student and clients, I began to write my first book: "Fly Fishing Women Explore Alaska." It was about six fly fishing locations in Alaska and the women I took to fish there with a fly rod.

As I and my editor expected, it was very difficult to find a publisher. One after the other turned it down, some saying that they weren't publishing fly-fishing books, and others coming right out to say they wouldn't publish a fly-fishing book written by a woman.

I finally got a small regional publisher to take a chance. To our amazement the "Fly Fishing Women Explore Alaska" turned out to be a great success and won a Silver Medal in the Benjamin Franklin Book Awards in 2004.

It wasn't long until I began to think about the need for an instructional book to introduce young women to the sport. Along the way it occurred to me that the book might have more appeal if it was partially written by some of the young women I had taught. Working on that idea I recruited Samantha, an Alaska girl, Alyssa, who lived and fished in the Midwest, and Blair and Alex, cousins from the East Coast, who became the "River Girls."

With the help of my pioneer collaborators and "co-authors" of the book, we went to work. I put together a list of questions for them to begin discussing what they already knew about fly fishing and what experience they had actually fly fishing. Using their replies and experiences we went on to create an introductory fly fishing book for beginners. That book won the Gold Medal in the Benjamin Franklin Awards in 2007.

These and other women and girls have come on the scene thanks to some enlightenment on the part of the fly-fishing industry and books like this, as well as an increase in women guides, classes, and fly-fishing clubs all around the country.

Now there is another era unfolding, led by a stellar young woman and her pioneering history in the fly-casting competition arena, previously dominated by men. We've welcomed this young champion, Maxine McCormick, to join the original River Girls in passing on their hard-won knowledge to new waves of sportswomen who come to appreciate the exciting challenges of this adventure.

Meet Maxine McCormick

By the time she was nine years old, Maxine McCormick was already into fly casting. Her family are members of the famous Golden Gate Angling & Casting Club in San Francisco, and that is where one of the casting instructors discovered Maxine's talents. Years before, her dad, Glenn, had taken her with him to the Fly-Fishing Show in Pleasanton, CA, where I had a booth, and introduced her to me. Little he or I would know that this delightful, tow-headed little girl would come to be a world champion fly caster just a few years later.

Maxine's dad also got her into fly fishing at the ponds at the club, but it wasn't until Donna O'Sullivan, a friend of her dad's and winner of fly-fishing competitions in her own right, gave Maxine some targets to cast at that she started playing games with them. After a month or so of casting that way, Donna introduced Maxine and her dad to the famous fly-fishing coach, Chris Korich, and it wasn't long until he took her on as a student. With Chris's guidance the prodigy began to enter (and win) various casting competitions, and the rest is history. She is now a gold medal winner in both national and international competitions.

Maxine says that Chris came to be like an extended family member to her. "He is not just there for me when it comes to fishing and casting, but for any time I need someone to talk to. I think that is what makes a good coach. He teaches me life lessons whenever I need it. He plays a big role in my life, and I wouldn't be who I am without him. He is an amazing caster who has an amazing ability to teach. I don't know anyone as dedicated to casting and as knowledgeable about it as him."

Chris says, "It's a special gift when a devoted teacher receives a young student that has all the natural "ingredients' and family support required to have a chance to become "the best" at something. Being entrusted to coach 9-year-old Maxine McCormick surely has been that special gift for me.

But more important than all the fly-casting secrets taught and ingrained, has been all the fun we've had over 5-plus years (casting, fishing, traveling) and the magical opportunity to mentor and pass on a bit of wisdom to a young person, growing and learning each day.

At times, I definitely practiced being a 'tough love' coach, but in Maxine's case, we both came to understand the importance of the fun over everything else, especially with our loving families and close supporters.

If becoming the youngest World Champion in sports history by age 12 were easy someone would have done it before Maxine. But I believe she's discovered a simple golden formula for other youngsters to follow. Find something you love to do, set clear goals, and have a lot of fun along the 'River Girls' journey."

Maxine says fly fishing is always fun for her because she is in nature and with people she enjoys. Those are her brother and dad, and sometimes her cousins and sometimes her friends. They are usually fishing, and she says that she loves the feeling of fighting a fish or watching one "slurp up" her fly. She says that since her dad and relatives only used fly rods, she never got into bait fishing or spin fishing.

A petite, delicate girl, still in high school, Maxine also competes in other sports with her friends. She runs cross country and track for her school, and also does some windsurfing with her mom. She says she likes that because it feels like she's flying.

Fishing as Well as Casting

Maxine started out fishing an eight-foot long rod, but now is fishing with an eight-foot, six-inch 5wt because that is the length of rod, she says she handles best. She says she likes to use floating lines for the same reason. When she's fishing, she uses a variety of dry flies, nymphs, and streamers, which are the flies that nearly every fly fisher uses routinely. She already knows that the fly to use is the one that the fish are the most interested in, based on time of day and the time of the year. Just recently Maxine has picked up a two-handed spey casting rod for distance competition.

"I totally recommend fly fishing to other young women," Maxine says. "Some of my friends have showed an interest since they know that I practice that sport. Fly fishing isn't just a male sport. Women can have just as much fun and be just as successful," she says. She likes teaching and helping people have fun fly fishing and says that she is totally open to showing other young women how to cast and how to fly fish.

"I think that just getting out on a river with people you like spending time with and a rod in your hand and ready to fish is always fun. Fishing is a release from everyday life and routines. The challenge of figuring out what the fish are eating and where they are holding makes it like a game or puzzle. Every time, it's different and exciting. Anyone who likes being in the outdoors and gives fly fishing an honest chance would enjoy it for their own reasons," Maxine says.

Maxime loves fly fishing as well as she loves fly casting. She calls that "fly-fishing without the fish," She usually fishes for trout, and at times for bass, but she hasn't caught a large variety of fish yet. She particularly likes sight-fishing, so she can use all of her casting techniques. "I don't really have a favorite place or fish. That is probably because there's so many places I want to travel and fish, and they're all different," she says.

Fly-fishing youth camps are taking place around the country now, and young people like Maxine have become a part of them. She has been going to the camp put on by the Redding Fly Shop in California since she was eight years old. Because she has had a very successful time there, she has gone again to the camp this summer for a week as a "Counselor in Training" with one of her friends. She hopes to go for an even longer stint next year.

The Sport of Fly Casting

The first fly cast that Maxine learned from Chris was the roll cast, which provided a solid base for many other casts such as the overhead, the side-arm, the double haul and the steeple cast. She remembers mixing training time in with fun time. When she was younger, she would take a break by climbing a tree or teaching her "critter toys" how to cast a fly.

Fly fishers know that they must learn to cast their fly rod correctly to get out to where the fish are. Overhead casting, roll casting, and side-arm casting are the three basic casts that most fly fishers try to master in order to catch fish. Various lengths and weights of rods, and matching floating or sink-tip lines, are usually sufficient for catching a particular species of fish. Various competitions in fly fishing require much more.

Fly casting competitions can be held in lakes or rivers, or at indoor water locations and are organized by various national or international organizations. Accuracy and distance are the two skills that are usually measured during casting competitions. Casting targets are hoops of different sizes, anchored to the bottom, that float on the water with other targets surrounding them. The angler casts to the hoops from an anchored platform. The different sizes of the hoops are worth different scores based on the rules of the competition. Competitors have five minutes to complete the course four times, left to right, and they accrue points depending on which ring they hit with their flies.

Distance competitions are ones that measure casts of different distances in the air with different gear and different rules. Maxine shines in both.

The national and world fly-casting competitions are usually held in the summer or early fall, which enables Maxine to manage her classwork even when doing her training time or traveling around the country and the world. Thanks to Chris, her coach, she is so diligent in her practicing that she is now competing with the adults.

Maxine's first win in a national championship was in Oakland, CA, in 2013 when she was just nine years old. Then came Tennessee in 2014, and Long Beach in 2015. Next was 2016 in Kentucky. These wins in the national competitions secure her a place on the Team USA, which competes in the world championships. Those were held in Estonia in 2016, where she won her first world gold medals in the women's trout accuracy event, and also shared the stage with her coach Korich, who won the men's world championship.

Her gold medal was truly an accomplishment, especially for one so young. The San Francisco Chronicle reported on August 7, 2017, that:

"Maxine McCormick, San Francisco's 12-year-old fly-casting prodigy, became the youngest gold medal winner at a world-class sporting event in history Friday. She tied her coach, Chris Korich of Oakland, for the gold and they became dual world champions at the World Championships of Fly Casting in Estonia.

While children have participated in world-class events, the previous youngest gold medal winner is believed to be 13-year old American diver Marjorie Gestring at the 1936 Berlin Olympics. Sixty-nine of the world's best fly-fishing casters from 15 countries are competing for medals in Estonia, located in the Baltic region of northern Europe. McCormick competed in an event called fly-casting accuracy, in which casters use fly rods, such as in the movie "A River Runs Through It" and then cast to small rings floating on pools. McCormick's father, Glen, won bronze for a medal sweep of the event by the San Francisco and Oakland Casting Club." She is now the most decorated fly -casting female of all time."

Competition in 2018

In 2017, the national championships in San Jose, CA were added to Maxine's list of victories. Also, on that list is the 2018 national tournament in Valparaiso, Indiana, which secured her membership on Team USA. This time the team headed out to the "big time" in the world championships of fly-casting held in Millom, England, with Maxine looking to defend the gold medals that she won in Estonia in 2016. One of those was in the women's trout accuracy event and the other was from a tie with her coach.

Maxine was determined to break her women's single-hand trout accuracy record in 2018, and break it she did, winning a gold medal with her record-setting cast of 161 feet, which set a new women's record. The second gold medal was for the 2-hand salmon distance event, which Maxine describes as her "favorite distance event." That cast was 189' feet long and brought the 2nd gold medal in the World Championships of Fly-casting in the UK to Maxine and Team USA.

Maxine's championship casts took place in winds gusting up to 40 miles an hour. This 14-year-old girl, just five feet, seven inches tall, picked up her custom fly rod (the one that her coach, Chris, had created for her,) gathered the fortitude built in hours and days of training, and made it happen! She even laid out a new women's distance record in the process. I can hardly imagine that, especially in those conditions.

To top it all off there was still another medal waiting to be won, and Maxine obliged. This time it was in the single-handed sea trout distance event. A cast of 161 in the qualifying round and a finals cast of 156 feet' brought her the silver medal. Maxine also defended her accuracy title with a score of 52 in the women's division -- 21 points ahead of the second-place finisher. What I would have given to have been there to see it all!

Its's back-to-back gold medals, for Maxine and the entire world is absolutely flabbergasted! Her latest fly-casting world championship demonstrates what a 14-year-old young woman with determination and excellent coaching can do in the world of fly-fishing competition. This competition included 123 casters from 20 countries. One of the international reporters called her, "America's Casting Princess." and a reporter for the New York Times has dubbed her "The Mozart of Fly Casting."

Maxine's Future

Being so famous at her young age doesn't seem to change Maxine's life. "I don't really think about it, and it doesn't really change anything except when someone at school searches for my name and finds out my accomplishments. I don't broadcast it and even when people do find out they think it is really cool, but it's not like I get treated differently," she explains.

Maxine thinks that she will keep on fly fishing competitively because she relishes it so much. She says "fly fishing is something I will enjoy for a lifetime. I have met so many people through fly fishing that I will have forever." She also has very supportive parents that she says, "are behind me in every decision I make about that." She thinks that she might move on to become a veterinarian or a pediatrician one day, but that she will never give up fly fishing in her life.

"I like the idea of getting more women interested in fly fishing. I think that girls and women can have fun with fly fishing and casting just like men. I would especially like to see more young girls learning," she declares. And the River Girls book will certainly help that along.

CHAPTER 2

What exactly is Fly fishing

Fly fishing is a special type of fishing. It's all about knowing what fish eat and finding ways to fool them with imitations of their food. The make-believe critters we use for fishing like this are called flies. Flies come in many different sizes, shapes, and colors. After we attach a fly to our line and toss it into the water, we hope a fish will decide to take a bite because our fake food looks yummy. That's when the fun begins.

You'll remember the first fish you catch with a fly for the rest of your fishing life. Once it happens, you're as hooked as the fish. An awesome sensation shoots up your arm when a fish grabs your offering. It's electric! Your heart pounds and your hand shakes. The fish tries to swim off while you try to reel it in. This is a test of wills and skills. Is the fish strong enough to get away? Are you smart enough to play him just right, so he doesn't escape?

The more successful you are in fooling fish with your fly, the more you want to fish, even when you don't win the contest. If the fish breaks off, you simply tie on another fly and try again. When you bring a fish next to you, where you can actually touch it and look into its eyes, the link between you is absolutely spellbinding. It's a moment to savor. If you carefully return the fish to the water, the two of you just might meet again another day!

Is Fly fishing Like Other Kinds of Fishing?

You may already know about the other two kinds of fishing-fishing with a spinning rod and fishing with a bait rod. In spin fishing, you have a metal lure or a plastic imitation of a worm or small fish tied to the end of clear nylon fishing line. To cast, you "wind up and pitch," slinging the lure out into the water where you hope the fish are waiting. In bait fishing, you use the same casting motion as in spin fishing, but there's a weight and a clump of fish eggs, a hunk of bait, or a worm on a hook tied to the line instead of a lure.

Fly fishing is more artful. You use a back-and-forth motion of the rod to

Use a back-and-forth motion to make the line sail out.

make the line sail out, sending a tiny, almost weightless imitation of a bug or a baitfish to the water to tempt your quarry. No smelly, gooey bait to deal with here. No heavy, dangerous three-pronged hooks to duck from, either. All three types of fishing focus on trying to get fish to eat what's on the end of your line, so that you can catch them. All three methods work.

In the beginning, only aristocrats fished for sport. Other people used nets or spears to get their fish and eat them. Much like subsistence fishers of today, they fished strictly for food and not for sport. The wealthy people who owned most of the land and the fishing waters had time on their hands to watch what the fish were eating and to think about how to catch them. They were the first to experiment with fur and feathers to create the imitation fish foods that we now call flies. They were also the ones who began creating different fishing rods.

Fishing with spin and bait rods came later, as sport fishing became affordable and popular with everyone. Many people now fish with these types of rods instead of with fly rods for two main reasons. First, spin and bait rods usually cost less to buy than fly rods. Second, slinging out a lure or a chunk of bait is easier than learning to cast a fly rod. Any fly fisher, though, will tell you that the challenge of casting is part of the fun.

What's Special About Fly fishing?

In a word, fly fishing is graceful. A fly rod is made longer than a spinning or bait rod, and it has a more delicate and flexible tip. This length and delicacy help zing the line out when you propel the rod back and forth in a certain way. Maybe you've seen people fishing with a fly rod and noticed the difference.

Flyfishers seem to be waving around an extra-long fishing rod to keep a large amount of line sailing through the air. That's because, in fly fishing, you're the one who must use the weight of the line to get it and the nearly weightless fly to go out onto the water. You don't have the heavy weight of a lure to pull the line out for you.

If you haven't seen people fly fishing on the river, maybe you've seen Brad Pitt in the movie A River Runs Through It. (No? Then make sure it's the next video you rent. It's sensational!) That movie beautifully shows what fly fishing means to a father and his two sons. Brad and the other actors all fish with fly rods. They demonstrate perfectly the lovely motions of casting a fly and the fun and excitement of catching a fish using a wispy bit of feathers.

Even though the two boys in the movie get frustrated as they learn to fly fish, it's not long before they turn into fly fishing fanatics. The same enchantment could happen to you, too. Fly fishing isn't just for guys, you know.

So, now you know what makes fly fishing different from other kinds of fishing. In the next chapter, we'll talk about how to get started, with some advice from our river girls.

The most special feeling you can imagine.

CHAPTER 3

Am I Ready to Fly-fish?

Yippee! You want to join your sister anglers and become a river girl. You'll find that fly fishing is a great way to be outdoors and that it brings a real sense of accomplishment.

So, how do you know if fly fishing might be a sport for you? Well, if you're a girl who enjoys nature, someone who likes spending time around water and who wants to learn new skills, you should definitely give fly fishing a try.

It may be that you have decided you're ready to learn fly fishing because you're tired of fishing with your spinning rod. Samantha, one of the river girls you'll meet in the next chapter, was like that.

Samantha

I fished with bait and spinners before I learned fly fishing, but anyone can throw out a lure or bait and catch a fish. Not everyone can throw out a fly and catch a fish. I'm the only one of my friends, including the guys, who knows how to fish with a fly rod.

I look forward to every summer just so I can use my fly rod again. When I'm out there on the river, it's so nice being alone, and when a thirty-inch rainbow takes my fly, that is the most special feeling you can imagine.

Perhaps you've seen someone else fly fishing and you want to try it because it seems more challenging than the fishing you've been doing. Or maybe you're lucky and know someone who's offered to teach you.

Another one of our river girls, Blair, started a little differently. Like Samantha, she had fished first with a spinning rod, but Blair hadn't really thought about switching until she was given the choice between fishing with a spinning rod or a fly rod during a trip to Alaska. She decided to try out fly fishing.

Blair

My cousin invited me to Alaska and informed me that we would be fly fishing at Brooks Lodge near a town called King Salmon. I was fourteen.

I had the choice to either use a spinning rod or a fly rod. I decided that fly fishing would be more enjoyable and would give me a real chance to test my fishing skills. My uncle helped me with the basics, and then our guide, Pudge, helped me with technique and taught me how to stay with the fish once I had it on the line.

Unlike our other river girls-Samantha, Blair, and Alex-Alyssa never really fished with a spinning rod or a bait rod before taking up fly fishing. She tried out all the different types of rods at about the same time but quickly settled on the fly rod as her instrument of choice. It was probably a combination of her mom's influence and that first fish that did it.

Alyssa
I never saw my mom fish with anything but a fly rod, and since I wanted to be as good a fly fisher as she was, that's the way I also chose to fish.

As the river girls prove, you can start fly fishing at almost any age. Blair was a teenager before she took up the sport, but Samantha, Alex, and Alyssa were fortunate enough to get to try it out before they were ten. So, no matter how old you are now, you can give it a try. You'll be surprised what a great outdoor activity it turns out to be.

No matter how old you are now, you can give it a try.

Can I Really Do This?

It's always a little scary to start something new, even if you're really excited about it. You've got to be brave just to show up at a fly fishing class where you might not know anyone and where you're not sure exactly what will happen. Going with a friend or with your folks will make you more confident. Were other girls scared at first? You bet.

Blair

I thought it was very hard to get a real feel for fly fishing. I was afraid my hands were going to get cut or the salmon was going to knock me over into the water. None of those things ended up happening. I was a lot worse at fishing than the people I was with at the time. They would be catching a fish every cast, when it would take me about an hour to even get a nibble. But I got pointers from people around me and ended up landing fish more frequently. I was also scared because the bears were around. It sent chills up my spine when we had to rip the fly away from the fish and move back whenever a bear appeared.

Samantha

When I started, I was afraid that I would hook someone or myself with the fly, and that still worries me sometimes.

As you can see, beginners are scared of different things when they start fly fishing. Because you'll practice first without a real hook on the end of your line, you won't have to be scared of snagging yourself or anybody else, like Sam was. You'll probably start with just a piece of bright yam tied to the line so you can see where your cast is going.

Many beginners are most scared of just looking silly, not knowing exactly what to do, not being sure they can ask questions, or not catching fish right away. That's pretty normal. Did you notice that Blair felt bad because at first everyone but her was catching fish? Well, she stuck with it, asked for help, and pretty soon was hooking up with the best of them. That sure did boost her confidence.

~

Learning to fly fish can also be confusing at first. In the next chapter, you'll learn from Alex that she wasn't so much scared as frustrated. That's the way most beginners feel, regardless of their age or sex. Still, she kept trying, and now she's enjoying the rewards.

"Don't get discouraged," Alex says. "There's a lot to master when you take up fly fishing."

Fly fishing is lots of fun!

Learning to fly fish is like learning any new skill. Whether you're learning to use a computer, learning to cook, learning to drive, or learning to use a checkbook, there are always periods of frustration, doubt, and worry. But most new things we learn are worth the effort it takes. Fly fishing certainly is. When you've acquired some of the skills, Samantha, Alex, Alyssa, and Blair promise you two things: that you'll feel a real sense of accomplishment and that it's lots of fun.

How Do I Get Started?

You should definitely take a fly fishing class or get some help learning the sport. Having a family member teach you is the way most girls start. That's what Alex recommends.

Alex

If it's possible, I think you should get taught by a family member, because it really allows you to get close to that person.

Now that moms as well as dads are fly fishing, everyone in the family has a chance to enjoy the sport. Alex learned from her dad, but you're just as likely to be learning from your mom, like Alyssa did. It used to be that mostly boys got to go fly fishing with their parents or other family members. That's all changing now, as more and more girls and women take part in sports of all kinds.

Certainly, some girls have been taught by guides or instructors who are paid by the hotel or ranch where their families are staying on a vacation, but there are many other free or low-cost options for getting started.

If you're a Girl Scout, fly fishing may very well be offered as one of the outdoor skills you could learn at summer camp. It's also possible that your school has a 'Trout in the Classroom" program where students go fly fishing. Or you might be able to take an environmental studies class that includes fly fishing. Fisheries education is often combined with classes like this to provide opportunities to try out fly fishing and/or fly tying.

Another way that you can locate free or inexpensive fly fishing programs for young people is to visit the web sites of Trout Unlimited (TU) and The Federation of Fly Fishers (FFF). Both of these organizations have chapters in your state, no matter where you live. Many of the chapters offer programs to help young people get started as Flyfishers.

Trout Unlimited's program is called "First Cast." Some clubs use their members to lead the workshops, and some offer sessions you can attend with your folks. Check out Appendix 3: Fly fishing Opportunities for Young People for some more ideas and web site addresses. Using an internet search like Google can also help you find programs in your area.

You might, for instance, live in an area where one of the many fly fishing clubs for women is located. Lots of them have sprung up around the country in the last few years. Some of those clubs offer special classes for girls, and some offer mother/daughter outings. A list of those clubs appears in the back of this book in Appendix 4: Fly fishing Clubs for Women.

If there is no club in your area, you can call a local fly fishing shop, sporting goods dealer, or outdoor store and ask them if they know a way for you to learn to fly fish. They may very well be offering classes, although there's often a charge.

Alyssa also has some thoughtful suggestions for you as you get started fly fishing. Lucky enough to have her mom as a teacher, she recommends that you find a woman to teach you, if at all possible. She says that maybe you and a couple of your friends could get together and locate someone to teach you as a group. That way, you'll also be sure to have someone to fish with afterwards.

Her other advice as you're getting started is not to frustrate yourself.

Alyssa

There's lots of complicated casts and knots and stuff to learn. You don't have to do it all at the start. Just learn enough at the beginning so that you can catch fish. Then expand your horizons later.

Women and girls are particularly good at fly casting because we have the grace and finesse to do it right. Our instincts seem to tell us not to force the rod forward as hard as we can or to use the "wind-up-and-pitch" motion that works for a spinning rod. You'll find more about casting techniques in Chapter 6.

What Equipment Must I Have?

As you get started, you'll probably be wondering where you'll get the equipment you need and whether it's going to be easy to cast a fly rod and make the line go out. You needn't worry. When it comes to fly fishing equipment, your instructor will have a rod and reel for you to use for your lessons. If your mom or dad is going to teach you, you can probably use equipment they already own.

Once you've learned to fly fish, you might be able to borrow equipment, or some stores in your area may have fly fishing equipment to rent. In time, you'll want to have your own rod and reel, but that usually comes later. When the time does come, you'll find lots of help in Chapter 4: Gearing Up: Fly Rod, Fly Reel, and Fly Line and in Chapter 5: Here Fishy, Fishy: Matching Up Fish, Gear, and Water.

How Easy Is It to Cast a Fly Rod?

As you will discover, it's really pretty easy to cast a fly rod and make the line go out, if someone teaches you how to do it. Fly casting is a technique, a skill, that has nothing to do with how strong you are or how far you can throw a ball. That's why anyone can do it with some basic coaching.

At the same time, fly casting isn't as easy as casting with a spinning rod. If you've fished with a spinning rod, you know that all you really have to do is wind up and pitch. Fly casting takes more concentration and more stick-to-itiveness. You may feel baffled at first, as Alex and Blair did, but that's true of most new skills you learn.

Blair

Fishing with the spinning rod was easier for me. It didn't involve much talent. I see that fly fishing has a wider range of fun and a wider range of learning.

Think about the first time you ever rode a bike or went skating. Were you able to keep your balance? How about the first batch of cookies you ever baked? Did they turn out just right? It probably will be the same with fly fishing. Don't worry,

Flycasting has nothing to do with how strong you are.

your teacher understands that it can be frustrating at first. Like Alex, Blair, and the other river girls, though, you'll discover just how much fun fly fishing really is if you stick with it.

Okay, so suppose you give it a try and decide you don't like it or it's too frustrating. If that should happen, just wait and try again another time. It's all right to decide that you'd just as soon continue fishing with your spinning rod for a while.

Of course, you might be a little hesitant to take up fly fishing or decide that you don't like it, if you have to go by yourself. If that's the case, find a friend (or two) who also thinks it sounds like fun and ask her to get started with you, as Alyssa suggests. Then, get going! The fish are waiting!

So, come on, let's meet the river girls next and begin exploring the wonders of fly fishing. In the chapters that follow, you'll hear some stories, find out about gear, and learn how you can get started wherever you live. Let's go fly fishing!

Alyssa, river girl.

CHAPTER 4

River Girls

ALYSSA

Some of Alyssa's earliest memories are of going fly fishing with her mom, Nancy, and a couple of her mom's friends. She can't remember exactly how old she was then. As close as she and her mom can figure, she must first have fished with a fly rod when she was around four or five years old.

At first, Alyssa admits, she didn't really cast the fly rod. Her mom would do that and then hand it to her. Her mom showed her how to hold the line correctly, together with the handle of the rod, and how to make little pulls on the line to keep the fly moving correctly in the water. It wasn't long until she was catching fish. "That first fish was really special," she says. "It was the first time I got to eat a fish I actually caught."

It doesn't matter that she can't remember exactly what kind of fish it was. It was the accomplishment that made it special. Her mom and friends caught fish all the time, and at last she felt as if she was "just like them."

Since Alyssa's mom is so passionate about fly fishing, it's no surprise that she introduced the sport to her daughter at a very early age. Nancy founded the Wading Women of Minnesota fly fishing club when Alyssa was just a tyke. She could hardly wait for her daughter to grow big enough that she could manage a fly rod. They've been fishing together ever since.

"What makes fly fishing extra special for me," Alyssa says, "is that I can do it with my mom. We laugh and call it our 'bonding time.'"

Even though her initial reaction to fly fishing was that it was exasperating, Alyssa persisted. Like all the other river girls, she reports being frustrated with tying on her fly, trying to get the line to go out, keeping her fly out of the trees, and with the other difficulties that every first-time fly fisher encounters. She guesses that the problem was partly "because I was so little." Not surprisingly, she says she even found that memorable first fish "yucky and slimy." Then she grins and adds, "I liked it anyway."

Bonding time with mom

Alyssa wasn't the only one who was frustrated, however. Her mom was also pretty confounded. She couldn't seem to keep Alyssa from wading into the deep pools on the river. At first, Alyssa seemed to have absolutely no fear of the water. A few scary dunkings, however, helped her learn about safe-wading practices.

Once she got started, Alyssa fished almost every time her mom fished. They are each other's favorite fishing partner. They've fished for bass and crappie, for Atlantic salmon and trout, and for a number of saltwater species, such as marlin, dorado, and rooster fish, while visiting Mexico.

One of the things Alyssa is still looking forward to learning is how to fish for different species in new places. She hopes they take some vacations to places that have other kinds of trout and maybe Pacific salmon.

"There are so many fish I haven't caught yet," she laments. Imagine, wanting to take a vacation in someplace other than Disney World or a dude ranch!

It was at the second annual festival of the International Women Fly Fishers (IWFF) where Alyssa and I first met. Because the festival was in Mexico where they have a condo, Alyssa and her mom had traveled up to the area known as East Cape, where the festival was held. Some of the other IWFF members had brought their children, and those kids usually played on the beach or at the pool. Alyssa was at the beach as well, but while the other kids were playing, she was casting her fly rod into the surf to see what fish she could catch. There she was when we came out of one of the meetings, a young girl in a bathing suit with a sunburned nose and braces on her teeth, excitedly telling us about the fish she'd caught. It was delightful.

Another day I remember waving goodbye to Alyssa and her mom and a couple of other women, as they set out on the boat to search for long-billed marlin, one of the most spectacular of all saltwater fish. She was definitely one of the group. She hasn't caught a marlin yet, but she's determined to do it one of these days.

"You'll love fly fishing," Alyssa promises. "It's very relaxing and challenging. Besides, you'll get a real charge when you catch your first fish."

SAMANTHA

A true Alaska girl, Samantha learned to fly fish at her mom's wilderness fishing lodge when she was just five years old. Having spent every summer of her young life at the lodge, she'd always been around fishing and fisher-people. She was destined to become a river girl.

Even before she could fish, she'd go along in the boat, wearing a tiny life jacket and soaking up all the activity like a sponge. Some of Sam's earliest memories are of standing on the bank and fishing for salmon, trout, and char right in front of the lodge. Before she learned to fly fish, she used a bait rod or a spinning rod. She has many pictures of herself as a very young girl holding fish nearly bigger than she was. An adult had to help her land her fish sometimes, but whenever possible, she wanted to do it herself.

Samantha, river girl.

Finally, the summer she turned five, one of the guides at the lodge gave her one of his old fly rods and began showing her how to use it. Many of the people at the lodge fished with a fly rod, and she'd been curious to give it a try to see what it was like.

"Fly fishing looked like more fun," she says. "I wanted to be able to fish like that, but everybody kept saying that I was too little."

31

It wasn't long before Sam was tying flies.

Sam nagged and nagged the guide until he relented and gave her a lesson. She took to it immediately and began trying to fish with a fly rod instead of her spinning rod whenever she and her mom got to spend time on the river.

Sam recalls that several of the clients at the lodge were impressed that such a young girl could do a basic cast with a fly rod. They thought it was neat that she was learning how to fly fish. That gave her incentive to stick with it. The fact that it may be more difficult to catch a fish with a fly rod than a spinning rod actually spurred her on to master fly fishing. Sam loves a challenge.

Sam and her mom, Claire, a widow at that time, returned to town each winter so they could be near other family members and so Sam could go to school. Still, much of the talk each day revolved around fishing. Plans took shape for the following summer, clients booked trips, and gear and equipment got organized. It was hard, Sam recalls, to leave her friends and her town activities and head out to the lodge each June, but she always looked forward to it because it meant being able to fish again.

It wasn't long before Sam was also tying flies. I gave her some of her first lessons and was surprised by her interest and concentration. Her mom, always trying to find ways to keep Sam occupied during the busy summer days, suggested that she tie some flies and sell them to the clients.

Soon Sam had a tiny "store" in the corner of the main room at the lodge where she displayed and sold her flies. The first time a client paid her a dollar for a fly, she was astounded.

"I thought they weren't good enough," she says.

Well, after that same client went out and caught several fish with her fly, he returned and commissioned more. She was ecstatic. Now she ties flies with skill and self-assurance. She's even appeared at outdoor shows demonstrating how to tie some of her favorites.

Now that she's older, Sam is more aware that running a wilderness lodge is pretty much a full-time undertaking and that her fishing has to wait until all the work is done. She has a summer job at the lodge as a kitchen helper and is quick to get the dishes done and the kitchen cleaned up each evening, so she'll be ready if she finds someone to go fishing with her. It usually doesn't take much prodding. Fishing is the life of the lodge. During June and July, the long hours of daylight in Alaska certainly provide more fly fishing opportunities than she'd get in most other places.

When I first got to know Sam, she was seven. Even then I found her to be one of the most persistent and tenacious anglers I knew. She'd stand patiently, casting again and again, never once whining if she wasn't catching fish. Instead, she was always quick with questions that helped improve her technique, her cast, or her understanding of where the fish might be. In fact, the only time I heard her complain was when she couldn't go fishing.

From then on, every time I came to the lodge to teach fly fishing for women, Sam and I managed to squeeze in a few opportunities to fish together. Her concentration and enthusiasm never failed to impress me. She'd ask about the flies, practice her casts, and catch lots of fish. Soon, she was also joining my clients, as they learned how to tie the knots that Flyfishers use to make the connection between the fly line and the fly.

SAM'S FAVORITE FISHING STORY

I caught lots of fish after I started fly fishing, but I really, really wanted to catch a king salmon. I kept explaining to my mom that the fly rod I had wasn't heavy enough to catch such a large fish, and I needed a stronger fly rod. Finally, we made a deal: I could have my own king salmon rod once I had actually caught my first king salmon on a fly.

One day, when I was ten, we were out in the boat, and there were lots of kings in the river. My stepdad, Dave, said I could use his ten-weight fly rod. Boy, was I ever excited. The rod was rigged with a sink-tip line and a Popsicle fly. I had some trouble casting it, because it was quite a bit heavier than what I was used to. I'd been using a floating line, and it was also more work to cast the sink-tip. You had to use a heavier line to get down to where the fish were, though, so I kept at it.

I was beginning to wonder if I could even hook up a king, let alone catch one, when a fish grabbed my fly. Wow, what a feeling! My heart was pounding, and my knees were shaking. I knew that I had a lot of work to do, if I was going to land it. I had to play the fish for twenty minutes before I finally got it in. "Playing" it is the wrong word, though. It was just plain hard work. I knew I had to let the fish run or it would break off. The whole time I had the fish on, I was switching hands back and forth on the rod, because my arms were getting tired. I also had to press my palm up against the reel to help slow the fish down. I'm glad it was the kind of reel where I could do that, or I might not have landed the fish.

Throughout the whole ordeal, I kept remembering the first time I learned how to palm a reel. Pudge had given me her rod with a fifteen-pound chum salmon that she'd hooked, so I could learn how to play a big fish. She'd shown me how to flatten my hand and press up from underneath the reel to slow down the turns of the spool. Once, though, I forgot as the fish zoomed around the river. The wind-knob on the reel ripped out of my fingers and hit my knuckles. Boy, did that ever hurt! Well, I didn't forget this time.

This salmon was going to prove to my mom that I needed a heavier fly rod. I just couldn't lose it! And I didn't! We finally got it in the net and into the boat. It seemed absolutely huge to me! The scale showed thirty-

Sam only complained when she couldn't go fly fishing.

34

five pounds when we weighed it. A quick whack on the head sent it to fish heaven, and we took it back to the lodge for dinner.

Mom said, "Way to go Samantha!" when she saw my fish. She was really proud of me, and I was really proud of myself. I got my new ten-weight fly rod the next spring.

Sam has caught over twenty more king salmon since that first one. Now she does it with that great new fly rod.

As Sam has become more involved in school activities, she hasn't been able to stay the entire summer at the lodge. She has had to head to cheerleading camp and return to Anchorage for school registration before the lodge closes. She's torn between knowing that she has to leave just when the best silver salmon and rainbow trout fishing occurs on the river and wanting to return to her friends and her school.

"Even though I probably get to fish much more than most girls, it still isn't enough," Sam says. "I don't think it ever will be."

ALEX

Montana, that legendary land of fly fishing, is where Alex first learned to fly fish. She was eight years old and remembers being on a school vacation with her family. Watching other anglers fish, she noticed that fly fishing seemed to be the best method to catch the fish and that her dad was really into it. She got interested because he seemed so enthused. When she said she'd like to try fly fishing, her dad took the time to begin teaching her. That was the start of something great!

After that first fly fishing experience in Montana, Alex began using a fly rod every chance she could. Accompanying her dad, she got to fish a lot.

"I found fly fishing quite frustrating at first," she admits, "because I kept getting my line and my fly snagged in the trees." Her previous fishing experiences with a spinning rod hadn't been nearly so difficult for her. "Another problem was that, as an eight-year old, I guess I had a pretty short attention span."

Alex admits to also being frustrated because she didn't catch fish right away. But none of that discouraged her. She loved the "quality time" she got to spend with her dad because she was interested in his favorite sport, so she persisted. Later, catching a lot of big fish helped, too.

Alex lives in Boston. She's a very athletic young woman, participating in activities such as gymnastics at her school. On most vacations, however, she and her family go fishing. That takes her to lakes and rivers in New Hampshire for different kinds of trout and to salt water in Florida. As a result, she's encountered lots of different species of fish and has had an opportunity to use light- and heavyweight rods for catching them.

Six years after her first attempt at fly fishing, Alex could list striped bass, rainbow trout, brook trout, cutthroat trout, small mouth bass, silver and sockeye salmon, bonefish, tarpon, and sailfish among the species she's pursued. That's quite a list for a fourteen-year-old. When I met Alex, she and her family were on a vacation to Alaska. Alex and her dad, along with her brothers and her cousin Blair, were fishing for sockeye salmon on the Brooks River in Katmai National Park in western Alaska. I was there, guiding a group of women fly fishers. We were all standing knee-deep in the crystal water, casting to hordes of salmon headed up the river to their spawning grounds. The river was absolutely seething with fish.

Alex's dad was striving mightily to keep four young people rigged up and fishing, while helping to release the fish they caught. At the same time, he was staying alert for any resident bears. Everybody was having a wonderful adventure.

That evening in the lodge, we got better acquainted and planned for Alex and Blair to fish with me before they left for the rest of their trip and before my next group of women arrived. Bright and early the next morning, both girls were raring to go and right on time, all decked out in neoprene waders and equipped with rods and reels rented from the lodge.

The fish were exactly where we'd left them the night before, just waiting for us. I helped the girls rig up their flies and put some small lead sinkers on their leaders. Both of them hooked fish almost as soon as they put their flies in the water.

"Wow, I got one!" Alex cried, as her rod bent with the weight of a feisty sockeye salmon. That fish knew just what to do, though, to quickly gain its freedom. Alex needed to set the hook more firmly in the fish's jaw before she would get a fish on that stayed on.

When the next fish bit, she made sure her fly was stuck in its mouth really hard so it couldn't get off. Alex had had some experience with large fish, so she knew she had to let the fish run after she hooked it. And run it did. Up the river and down, this fish was a real speedball. Thanks to Alex's patience, though, it finally tuckered out, and she reeled it in. The fish was a beauty! Sleek and silvery, it was a perfect example of the salmon that every Alaska visitor dreams of.

Since Alex doesn't like to kill fish, I removed the hook for her and she knelt patiently at the water's edge, gently cradling her fish as the current flowed through its mouth and it revived. She had definitely learned the proper technique for practicing catch-and-release. (You'll find guidelines for practicing catch-and-release in Chapter 14: You Are the Future.)

As soon as the fish darted off, Alex was back to fishing before I could even get up off my knees. When a large, brown, four-legged fisher appeared on the far bank, both girls quickly reeled in their lines. On this river, bears have the right-of-way, so when this one came looking for his lunch, the three of us backed out of the water and headed up to the observation platform. As we stood there with a uniformed Park Service ranger, the girls discovered that it was nearly as much fun to see the bear fish as to be fishing themselves.

The bear stared intently at the school of fish, and when just the right moment came, he leapt into the seething mass with jaws ready to close around a slippery body. It was pandemonium! The fish were doing anything and everything to get out of his way.

Soon the bear's head emerged from the water with a flopping fish clenched in his teeth. Then he retired to the grassy bank for brunch. It was a while before he finished up and left. Only then could we return to our fishing.

ALEX'S FAVORITE FISHING STORY

It was spring break of 1997, and I was lucky enough to be in Florida. Instead of just sitting at the beach or at the pool and being lazy, I went out fishing with my family as much as possible. On this particular day, it was too windy to go out to the reefs, so we went to the flats to try for bonefish. I'd never even tried to catch one of those, so I was really excited. We got to the "top secret bonefish spot" after a long, windy drive. Since I was not very experienced at fly fishing then, my dad rigged up the lines and flies.

At first, my dad would cast, and I would strip the line in, but I decided I wanted to try by myself. My first few casts were not very good, but I finally began to get the hang of it. I waited until we saw a school of bonefish and then cast toward them. It may have been just luck, but I hooked up! My dad held my waist to make sure I didn't get pulled into the water.

I started to strip in, but my dad told me the fish was going to be a fighter. I knew what to do-pull the rod up and wind on the way back down-and I did exactly that. The fish fought like crazy and the line went screaming out. I waited patiently. When the fish stopped, I wound in as fast as my ten-year-old hands would allow.

After fighting this "monster" fish for about twenty minutes, I finally got it in. The fish was only ten inches long! That isn't very big, but I was happy to have caught a bonefish at all. My dad told me that bonefish are really hard to catch, and that made me even happier. We took a picture, of course, and then the boat captain put the fish back into the water. I was so proud of myself! It was my very first saltwater fish on a fly, and I had done it all by myself. To this day, catching that little bonefish is one of the most memorable of all my catches.

These days Alex fishes with her dad and by herself in New Hampshire's lakes and rivers, as well as in Florida in the ocean and in Boston Harbor near where she lives. Lately she has added stripers to the list of fish she's caught. She says this to other young women about fly fishing:

"Fly fishing is such a great skill to know. It is really fun to learn, and it's an exciting sport. You don't get judged by anyone based on your skill in the sport. Fly fishing lets you step away from the world and just be yourself."

BLAIR

From the time she was seven or eight years old, Blair fished with a spinning rod. She'd cast off the dock at the family's lake-front cabin in New Hampshire. Even though she didn't consider herself much of a fisher, she'd caught several different species, including trout, bass, and sunfish, by the time she was a teenager.

Since her folks aren't anglers, she'd mainly fish when she was with her cousins. They pretty much got her rigged up, helped her get her fish in, and functioned as her teachers and experts.

"I really enjoy being with my cousins," she says. "And, I love fishing for fun." Even though she probably didn't know it at the time, she was ready for fly fishing.

When she was fourteen, Blair and her cousin, Alex, traveled to Brooks Lodge in Alaska to do some bear-watching and some fishing. As they watched people fishing for salmon on the Brooks River, she noticed that many of the most successful anglers were using fly rods. That helped her decide to give fly fishing a try.

As they got started fishing, her uncle, Alex's dad, helped her with the basics of casting. He tied a fly on for her and helped her get positioned where the fish were. Since her three cousins also needed assistance, she couldn't rely on his help all the time, however.

"It was pretty frustrating at first," Blair reports. "I thought it was very hard to get a feel for it." Like most beginning fly anglers, Blair got her line tangled, had fish get off, and had trouble getting her fly out where she wanted it. The hardest thing was seeing other people catch fish when she couldn't.

"I couldn't even get a nibble, when they were all hooking fish," she says.

Blair could have taken the easy way out and gone back to using a spinning rod, but she didn't. She decided that she was going to master this fly fishing thing and kept at it. That's often what it takes to become a fly fisher. Well, her persistence paid off, and pretty soon she too was hooking up.

When Blair and I got to fish together the following day, I showed her how to keep the fish she was hooking on her line and how to stay with the fish and play it once she had it. She quickly learned how to let the fish run and then to reel him in when he rested. Wow, was she ever proud when she finally landed her first salmon on a fly rod!

The abundance of sockeye salmon at the Brooks River during her visit increased her chances dramatically. She certainly had a lot of fish to practice on. As her confidence built, she found she wasn't nearly so worried about things like falling in the water or having the line cut her hands, and she really began to enjoy herself. Actually, managing to land fish became the frosting on the cake.

"A spinning rod is easier to fish with and doesn't involve much talent," Blair says." Fly fishing definitely has a wider range of both fun and learning."

Not only was it fun, but where she was fishing, it was also pretty exciting and educational.

"Seeing the bears at the Brooks River was fantastic!" Blair says. "What a thrill!"

Having such a thrilling opportunity to see the bears fishing for the same salmon that she was, Blair also learned a very important lesson about what fish provide to others in our natural world. She realized that the bears need the fish to survive and that we humans must put our fun aside at times and not interfere with their fishing.

"I was pretty lucky to have first started fly fishing in Alaska," Blair says. „I mean, really, who would've thought that would be the first place someone would go fly fishing?"

Now that she has started fly fishing and has found out what fun it really is, Blair and Alex are always on the lookout for more places where they can go fly fishing together.

"I'd recommend fly fishing to other girls because it is a great way to be outdoors, have some fun, and then walk away with a smile on your face," Blair says.

PART TWO

Basics First

Your flyrod, line, and reel must match.

CHAPTER 5

Gearing UP: Fly Rod, Fly Reel, Fly Line

J ust like any other sport, fly fishing requires its own special equipment. You'll need a fly rod (notice that Flyfishers don't call it a "pole"), a matching fly line, and a reel that is the correct size to hold the line and help balance the rod. That's the basic setup. In this chapter we're going to help you understand how rods, reels, and lines work together.

Most likely you will start out using fly fishing equipment that your mom or dad has or that you use in a class you're taking. After a few lessons and some practice, you'll likely decide you're ready for a rod and reel of your own. In the pages that follow, you'll find some great tips on what to look for and ask about when you go shopping. In this chapter, the river girls and I will give you some ideas about how to pick the right equipment for the fish you want to catch and the water where you plan to fish. In the next chapter, we'll go into more detail about how to match up all the parts.

FLY RODS

Let's start with fly rods. A fly rod is longer, more tapered, and more flexible than either the spinning rod or the bait-casting rod that you might have been fishing with up to now. Those features help make the line go out as you cast. There are three important features of your rod: its length, the size of line the rod is designed to cast (or line weight, as it's called in fly fishing), and its "action"-where and how it bends and flexes.

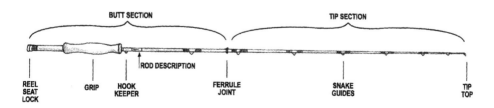

Parts of a fly rod.

Rod Length

Fly rods can be anywhere from six feet long up to fourteen feet long. A rod that is eight to nine feet long is the best for most kinds of fly fishing. You can use that length rod to fish from the bank, in the surf, or from your float tube or canoe.

As a general rule, if you're under five feet tall, you will probably be more comfort able casting a rod that is eight or eight-and-a-half feet long. If you're five feet tall or more, a rod that is eight-and-a-half or nine feet long is preferable. These aren't hard and-fast rules. Try out rods of those lengths and see how you like casting each one before you decide which to buy.

Line Weight

This feature of a fly rod is the one that people find the most baffling when they start fly fishing. Line weight tells what size of fly line the rod is designed to cast. True, it sounds a little odd to describe a rod by the weight of the line, but that's just the way the system has been for many years and we're stuck with it. The correct line weight for a specific rod is indicated right on the rod, so that helps a

ROD/LINE WEIGHTS FOR DIFFERENT FISH

Rod Length	Line Weight	Types of Fish	
		Freshwater	Saltwater
8-9 ft.	4-6	rainbow, cutthroat, brown, and brook trout; bass; bluegills; crappie; pink salmon; Dolly Varden; Arctic char; Arctic grayling; and similar fish	surf fish
8-9 ft.	7-9	Atlantic salmon; Pacific salmon including: pink, silver, sockeye, and chum; steelhead; northern pike; muskie; large bass or trout; bonefish; striped bass; redfish	Atlantic salmon; Pacific salmon including: pink, silver, sockeye, king, and chum; rooster fish; bonefish; dorado (mahi-mahi); jack cravalle; bonito; redfish; small tuna; striped bass
8-9 ft.	10-14	large king salmon, large Atlantic salmon	large king salmon, large Atlantic salmon, marlin, sailfish, large dorado, tuna

Note: Salmon can be fished for in both fresh and salt water.

lot. It may say "#5 Line," for example, meaning that rod casts a five-weight line the best. Because of this system, that rod would be referred to as a "five-weight rod."

Lighter rods (and their matching lighter lines) have numbers from four-weight to six-weight. They are used to catch fish such as trout, crappies, bluegills, and bass. (There are rods and lines from one-weight to three-weight, but they're difficult to cast.) You will probably use a six-weight rod when your folks teach you to fly fish or when you take a class.

Stronger rods are used to cast heavier lines, from seven-weight to fourteen-weight. They are used for bigger, fatter, stronger fish. An eight-weight rod could be used to catch steelhead or pike. A ten-weight rod would be needed for king salmon and a twelve-weight rod for marlin out in the ocean. Here's a chart to help you keep it all straight.

As you can see, your rod should be matched to the size and type of fish you're after. When you select a rod for yourself, decide what kind and size of fish you're going to fish for the most and then choose the rod and matching line weight that is right for that fish. If you have questions, ask for help. We'll talk much more about that in the next chapter, where you'll also find out what the river girls have learned about rods.

Rod Action

Besides just deciding on what rod length and line weight you need, it's also important to know how a rod will bend or flex when you cast it and when you're using it to fight a

Fish. The rod's action can make a difference in how tired you get when you're casting all day, and it can help or hinder you in landing big fish.

You can't see "action" or "flex" when you're looking at a rod, but most fly rod manufacturers now have a chart in their catalogs to show you how and where the rod bends. The illustration here is an example.

Each rod manufacturer has a different way of describing flex, so before you buy a rod, I recommend that you step outside with the sales person from the fly shop and try out the rod. See how it feels when you cast it. Also have the salesperson pull on the line to imitate a fighting fish, so you can see how the rod bends. The action of a fly rod has a lot to do with your fishing success, as well as with your casting comfort.

Here's a chart you can refer to for help in understanding the different types of action. As you can see, the rods that have a medium or a medium-fast action are probably the best for you.

UNDERSTANDING FLY ROD FLIES

Type of Action	How Much of the Rod Flexes	Easy to Cast?	Advantages	Recommended for You?
Fast-action or tip-flex	Only the very tip	No	Experienced casters get longer casts	No
Medium-fast action	About 1/4 of the way down from the tip	Fairly	Increased casting distance, helps land large fish	Yes–the best for you if you fish for large fish
Medium action	About 1/3 of the way down from the tip	Yes	Most comfortable to cast all day	Yes–the best rod for average-size fish
Slow-action	About 1/2 of the way down from the tip	No	None–They're usually quite wobbly	No

When you have a salmon, redfish, or northern pike on your line, they're going to be big and fast. Your rod must be able to help you fight them. The bottom two-thirds of a medium-fast rod (down through the handle) is stiff and strong to help you control big fish, but the rod is still pretty easy to cast all day. For everything from bluegill to average-size trout and bass, a medium-action rod will be best for you.

Models and Costs

Fly rods, no matter what length they are, come in two-piece models or in multi-piece models with three, four, five, six, or even seven pieces. These multi-piece rods are great for backpacking or for fitting your rod in an airplane's overhead bin, but they're more expensive.

Fly rods these days are made of graphite, a lightweight but very flexible material. You can expect that the more expensive a fly rod is, the more advanced is the graphite with which it is made. Better-quality rods also come in a soft cloth "sleeve" for protection from scratches, and they come with a carrying case or tube, as well. That's usually made out of metal or PVC pipe, so you can travel with the rod or store it safely when you're not using it.

Fly rods can cost as little as $40 at some large chain stores or as much as $600 at fly fishing shops. Based on the shopping possibilities where you live, you may also want to look at some catalogs or on-line stores for your equipment. The

The action of a fly rod has a lot to do with your fishing success.

drawback is that you can't try out a rod before purchasing it, so check out their return policies in case you don't like the rod.

Some starter rods come packaged with a fly reel and fly line so you can buy the whole setup at one time. They are usually referred to as "combos" or "outfits" and are available from shops in your community, as well as catalogs and on-line stores.

Unless you plan to fish for large fish, most of these starter packages will work just fine for you. Quality outfits run in the $150-$200 range for the whole set. Check out the rod's length, line weight, and action, and if it doesn't meet the criteria laid out in the charts we've given you, look a little further. Shopping at fly fishing shops or sporting goods dealers known in your community for their fly fishing products and expertise are usually your best bet to find a good range of options. Plus, you can actually try things out.

Now, let's move on to your reel.

SOME MANUFACTURES OF FLY FISHING COMBOS

Manufacturer	Rod/Reel/ Combos	Line Combos with Accessories
L.L. Bean	X	
Scientific Angler	X	
Cabela's	X	X
Cortland	X	
Bass Pro Shop	X	

Fly Reels

There are three major considerations in choosing a fly reel. First, it must be large enough to hold the size of line that your rod is supposed to cast, plus some extra line called "backing." Second, it should not be any larger than it needs to be, because that will add weight that will tire you out more. It may also affect the balance of your rod. Third, it must have a good drag system to help you fight a big fish you've hooked that's headed down the river.

First, let's learn the parts of a reel.

Fly rods are made of graphite, a lightweight but very flexible material.

Parts of the Reel

A fly reel has two extenstions called "feet," used to attach it to the rod, a main section called the "reel base," and a part that holds line and turns, called the "spool." The spool clicks into the base and then revolves as it lets line out or reels it in.

There's a small handle on the spool to help you wind it. After you've hooked a big fish that takes line out, keep your fingers away from the handle, or it will rap your knuckles as it spins around. Wind the handle only when the fish is resting. Let the drag of the reel help you keep control of the fish until it decides to rest.

Alex

As I've gained experience with different kinds of fish, I've also become familiar with different rods, reels, and lines. When I started fly fishing, I kept forgetting to let go of the wind knob on the reel when the fish was running. It really hurt when the knob hit my knuckles.

You can wind your reel with either your right or your left hand. Neither way is right or wrong. Try out both to see which is more comfortable for you. If you decide that you want to cast and reel with the same hand, then you'll have to switch the rod over to your other hand when you're playing a fish, so that you can reel it in. Don't worry, that's not a big problem. Just don't switch hands while the fish is running, or you might drop your rod. Wait until the fish rests, then switch, and you're ready to wind.

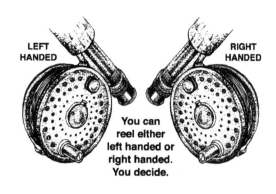

LEFT HANDED

RIGHT HANDED

You can reel either left handed or right handed. You decide.

You should decide which hand you want to wind with before you buy your reel, so you can tell the people at the store when they put the line on your reel. If you forget, it might not wind the way you want it to. If you decide to reel one way and later change your mind, just take your reel back to the shop and ask them to switch it. They will, and there is usually no charge.

Reel Sizes

Information that comes with the reel from the manufacturer will tell you what rod and line weight it should be used for. The information will also include something about the "backing" and what size and how much should be put on the spool. Backing is a flat, woven Dacron line that is wound on the spool before the fly line is put on. It helps to fill up the spool to the right dimensions, and it also gives you extra line if your fish should run so fast and so far, that it pulls out all of your fly line.

Following the reel manufacturer's recommendations will assure that the reel isn't too heavy or too light for the rod that you're going to put it on. A rod and reel have to balance for you to cast well.

Reel Weight

Your reel should be lightweight so that you don't get tired casting it all day. That's one reason you should make sure you get a reel that's the right size for your line weight and rod. Put different reels that are designed to hold the same size line in your hands at the same time. You'll quickly see which one is lighter, but don't automatically choose it. Some lightweight reels may not have a strong enough drag for the fish you're going after. It is very important for your reel to combine light weight and good drag to perform well. Some reels are also maintenance-free, which makes taking care of them a snap.

Drag

Besides being the correct size, your reel has to have something called "drag" to help you land a fish. Drag is resistance the reel exerts on the line as it is being pulled out. It helps you put the brakes on to slow down your fish. Drag may not be a big deal if you're catching average-size fish, but without it, a big bass will run amok! You should have drag on your reel that is strong enough to hold the fish that you might catch as well as the fish you intend to catch. Obviously, for larger fish, you're going to need more drag.

Blair

I sure wish I'd had more drag on my rented reel when I was trying to land my salmon. I think the reel was only set up for trout.

Because it's difficult to see this thing called drag, ask your mom or dad or your instructor or a salesperson to show you a reel with line already on it and to demonstrate how the drag works. The amount of drag a reel applies to the line is adjustable, and you should ask to see how you'd tighten or loosen the drag. Usually a knob on the back of the reel makes it tighter or looser. Now, you pretend to be the fish. Pull on the line so that you can see how strong the drag on the reel is when it's tight and when it's loose.

Cost of Reels

If you buy a reel separately, you can expect to pay $100 to $150 for a quality one, depending on the size of rod you want to match it up with. A saltwater reel should have an anodized finish to keep it from eroding and may be more expensive. Don't forget to check out the guarantee or warranty to make sure that any defects are covered and that the manufacturer will repair it if necessary. A good reel is worth the investment, because it will last you a long, long time.

Fly Lines

Fly lines are fat and slick. They are very different from the monofilament line you use on your spinning or bait-casting rod. They're made that way so that they slide out along the rod guides more easily when you cast.

Most fly lines are about eighty-five to ninety feet long. They come in lots of different colors. The fish won't see the fly line when you're fishing, because it's separated from the fly by the leader, which we'll discuss in Chapter 7. So, you can choose any color you like. You can expect to pay about $50 to $60 for a good fly line. Fly lines are created with something called "taper." That means some sections of the line are fatter than others. The fly line you'll use most is a floating line with what is called a "weight-forward" taper. Look on the package to make sure that's the type of line you're buying and then have the shop put the line on your reel for you. And don't forget to tell them which hand you've decided to wind with.

In addition to floating lines, there are also lines that sink or sink only at the tip. We'll talk about them in the next chapter.

Fly lines last many years, if you take care of them. That involves using a substance that not only cleans your line but also restores its slick surface. Once or twice a year, you just pull out the line and wipe it with a pad that is coated with a special cleaner. When you're finished, just wind the line back up. That's all there is to it.

Fly lines: choose any color you like.

So, there you have it. With the information in this chapter you've learned how a fly rod works, how to choose your fly rod, reel, and line, and the correct names for different parts of your equipment. In the next chapter, we'll give you even more information about matching the equipment to the fish you're trying to catch and the type of water you're fishing.

After that chapter, you should be prepared to get all the right equipment. When you're ready to buy, see Appendix 1: A Shopping Guide for Gearing Up for a shopping checklist and more information on gear.

CHAPTER 6

HERE FISHY, FISHY
MATCHING UP FISH, GEAR AND WATER

In the last chapter we explained the basic equipment you'll need in order to fly fish: a fly rod, a fly reel, and a matching fly line. In the beginning you'll probably be using someone else's setup, so they'll already have it correctly rigged for you. But, suppose you're now ready to get your own. Well, your decisions about equipment are going to be determined by two things: what type of fish you're going after and where and how you're going to be fishing.

What Fish Are You After?

Knowing what fish you're after will guide you to the rod and the reel you should buy. You can use a lighter rod for bluegills, crappie, and most bass and trout fishing than you would need for larger fish, such as salmon, steelhead, pike, bass, and redfish.

Go back to our chart in Chapter 4 that shows the rod lengths and line weights for different fish to find the kind of fish that you'll be fly fishing for. (If your kind of fish isn't on the chart, find one that is similar in size and weight or ask for help.) The chart will give you an idea what rod and line weight to use for that fish.

The heavier the line weight of the rod, the larger the fish it can be used to catch. Remember that your reel must be able to hold the size of line that matches your rod. More about reels and fly lines later, but now let's start with some more information about rods for average-size fish.

Rods for Average-size Fish

If you'll be fishing for bluegills, sunfish, perch, and small bass, trout, or grayling most of the time, then you might want to buy a four-weight or five-weight rod. A lightweight rod makes catching fish of this size lots of fun, because you can really feel what the fish is doing on the end of your line. The lighter weight of these rods makes them easy to cast on an all-day adventure, too.

Most people who are going to fish for small and average-size fish buy a five-weight or six-weight rod. That enables them to use the rod for a wider range of fish. They can still enjoy bluegills and crappies, but their slightly heavier rods will be good for larger cutthroat trout in Montana's big rivers or a lunker bass from a lake in Ohio.

Landing a really large trout or bass on any of these lightweight rods can be challenging. They aren't as strong as heavier rods, and you'll need patience and skill to bring in a really large fish.

Alyssa had some good opportunities to try out various rods, reels, and lines. She learned to fly fish using a six-weight rod and says that it was "a little heavy for a fiveyear-old." But that's what her mom had, so that's what she tried. Because they were fishing for trout, it was the correct size. Since then, she's used much heavier rods for larger fish.

Even though she goes after larger fish sometimes, Alyssa fly-fishes a lot for the trout in the lakes or streams near her home. Because there's a variety of fish near where she lives, she's probably fished for nearly every type of average-size fish that you could think of.

Other girls who have started fly fishing already have also told me that they have lots and lots of fun fishing nearby ponds for the sunfish, bluegills, and bass that live there. I've met girls at fly fishing events who tell me that they have already caught six or seven different kinds of fish on a fly rod, because they have lots of places where the Department of Fish and Game in their state stocks rivers and ponds with species that are just perfect for learning to fly fish.

Fish don't have to be big for you to have a great time fly fishing, especially on a lighter rod. Every fish has its own special beauty and its own special fun. Try them all.

Rods for Larger Fish

Samantha has experience with a number of different fly rods. She's lucky enough to spend her summers on a river that supports a variety of sizes of fish. Over time, she's assembled quite an array of rods to fish for them.

Samantha

I have various rod weights because I fish for a wide variety of salmon. I have a ten-weight for larger fish like kings and sometimes chums. I use an eight-weight for silvers, reds, and pink salmon. I use my five-weight for rainbows, grayling, Dolly Varden, char, and whitefish here in Alaska.

Nearby ponds provide fun fishing for bluegills and bass.

Alex also has experience using many different sizes of rods, though they're not all her rods. She's fished lots of places. She's also fished for lots of species, including salmon, trout, striped bass, smallmouth bass, bonefish, tarpon, and sailfish.

Alex

Since I fish for many different kinds of fish, I've fished with both heavy and lightweight rods. When we fished for sailfish, I used the heaviest rods on the boat.

Blair was using a rented seven-weight rod for the sockeye salmon we were catching in Alaska. Even though she hadn't had as much fly fishing experience as either Sam or Alex, she knew that she had to fish with a larger rod than she would use for the sunfish and bass that live near her home.

If you're going for those saltwater fish or for thirty-pound king salmon, like Samantha does in Alaska, then you'll need a ten-weight fly rod. Or if you'll be fishing for sailfish, like Alex does, you'd probably want a twelve-weight rod. Even an eight weight just wouldn't be strong enough to haul in either of those monsters.

The standard rod for most larger fish, however, is an eight-weight rod. It's as strong as you'll need for nearly everything, and you won't get so tired casting it.

Sam uses an eight-weight rod for salmon.

Rods for Both Average-size and Larger Fish

What if you plan to fish for both average-size and large fish? Most people can't afford to buy a rod for every size of fish they might fish for. Instead, they get the rod and reel that is right for the size of fish they'll be fly fishing for most of the time.

If that's a lightweight rod and they have an opportunity to fish for something larger, they borrow a heavier rod or rent one, until they can afford to buy a second rod of their own. That's the best strategy. If their regular rod is heavier, they can still use it for smaller fish, although it would be more fun to borrow or rent a lighter rod to use.

If you continue fishing a lot as you get older, you'll probably end up with two rods, one for smaller fish and one for bigger fish. That makes

Play a big fish carefully to land it safely.

it easy to match the rod to the size of fish you're after. In the meantime, it's good to be prepared for the fish you might catch as well as the one you intend to catch. That sometimes means knowing how to land a large fish on a light rod.

If a big bass should take your fly while you're fishing with a lightweight rod for its smaller cousins, don't panic. Just remember that you'll have to play the fish carefully, let it take out line, and really take your time in order to protect your rod and to land the fish safely.

Although what you're going to fish for is the most important issue for selecting your rod and reel, where you're going to be fishing is often the most important question for making other selections.

Where and How Will You Fish?

The question of where to fish can often be answered by the person who teaches you. The fly fishing class or workshop you attend may be held right on a river or lake where the fishing is known to be good.

Most people find good fly fishing spots in one of four ways:

1. They call up their state's Department of Fish and Wildlife, Department of Outdoor Recreation, or an agency with a similar name and ask for booklets or published lists of good fishing locations. These offices will send lots of materials, usually for free.

2. They talk to the people at a fly fishing shop or sporting goods store near where they live to get advice about where the fishing is good.

3. They ask friends or people in the fly fishing club their family belongs to about good places, or they may go with the club on a fly fishing outing.

4. They read books that tell about good places for fishing in their state or region. The library will help you here, or you can go on the internet and search for books about fishing where you live.

You can do any or all of these things yourself. It's easier than you think. Once you get an idea of the possible fishing spots, ask yourself which of them you think you'll be fly fishing most of the time. Will it be lakes, rivers, or salt water?

Fishing locations have different conditions, and you may have to fish each in a different way. For instance, lakes don't have currents and are deeper than most rivers. Saltwater fishing from the shore means you'll have to contend with surf and waves. You can learn to fish effectively in all those places from the people you go fishing with.

Let's look at lakes, rivers, and salt water one at a time to see how the water you fish affects your choices, such as the type of fly line and the flies you'll decide to use.

Lakes

In lakes, you have to decide whether you're going to use a fly that floats on the surface of the water or fish deeper. You'll make that decision based on what other people recommend or what you see happening. If you see "rings" on the surface caused by fish feeding, then you'll probably fish with a floating fly. If you don't see "rings," you'll most likely decide to fish under the surface.

If you're going to fish on the lake's surface or just a little bit under the water, you'll be using a fly line that floats. Sometimes you'll need to fish more than just a few feet below the surface, and then you'll need a fly line that has a sinking tip so you can get down to where the fish are. (More about sink-tip lines later in this chapter.)

Since people don't always know ahead of time where the fish will be feeding in lakes, they often take along both a floating line and a sink-tip line. They do that by buying an extra spool for their reel to put a second line on, something we'll discuss later in this chapter. That way they can switch spools, depending on what the fish are doing. Because there may be some very big lake trout, pike, bass, or rainbows lurking in the depths, keep in mind that you might catch a larger fish than you expect. Play it carefully and slowly and enjoy the thrill.

There are probably more ponds and small lakes in your neighborhood or town than you think. They are great places to start fly fishing. They often have lots of very cooperative fish, and they provide a place that you can go with a friend for an hour or two of fly fishing fun.

Ponds and small lakes are great places to start fishing.

Rivers

Rivers can hold as many surprises as lakes. We frequently go to a river for one type of fish, only to encounter something else. When we're fishing for trout, we might hook up with a whitefish. In what we think is a river with only smallmouth bass, we might end up with bluegill or even a catfish.

By selecting your fly carefully and by fishing at correct depths, you can often choose the kind of fish you catch. Ask other Flyfishers where in the water the fish you want to catch are likely to be and what fly to use. Small mouth bass, for instance, will come to the surface for a floating fly or a popper, but catfish won't. They want their food on the bottom.

Whatever fish you're after, in rivers you will most frequently fish with a line that floats. With that line, your fly can float on the surface, or you can get it at least a few feet under the water by using a weight on the leader or a weighted fly. Only rarely, in rivers with water six feet deep or deeper, might you need to use a sink-tip line.

Large rivers and small creeks are both exciting places to go fly fishing. No matter where you live, there are bound to be some of both not too far away. It's fun to practice drifting your fly along with the current when you're fishing water that is moving, and it's always interesting to find out what fish are in rivers and where they hide out.

Surf

Girls who live along the coastline typically fish in the surf. This is a type of fly fishing that is becoming more popular all the time. Many kinds of saltwater fish can be found just off the beach or shore. You can catch them on a fly by casting into the surf.

While fishing in lakes or rivers is fairly predictable, you never know what you're going to catch in the surf. In fact, that's one of the reasons people like

Rivers and creeks are both exciting places to go fly fishing.

to fish there. Sure, Flyfishers target redfish or rooster fish or surf perch when they know they're available, but they often catch something unexpected instead. Again, a certain fly may be especially good for a certain fish, but you still could connect with any one of several varieties of fish.

Many saltwater Flyfishers stick with floating lines to fish the surf. After all, they figure, the schools of bait fish are right near the surface of the water, so the bigger fish will come up to get them there. Besides, saltwater flies are often heavy enough so that they sink a little just by themselves.

Saltwater Flyfishers who believe that the line has to be heavy enough to sink through the breakers prefer a sink-tip line. A lot of surf fishing is done around rocks, though, so using a sink tip line can be tricky. It's easy to get hung up in the rocks if the tip sinks too much or too fast.

Ocean

When you fly fish out in the ocean, you face some of the same problems and choices that surf anglers do. Often, way out to sea, the fish you're after are chasing schools of bait fish right on the surface. Other times, the big fish are deeper, and you have to get your fly down to where they are.

Most saltwater (or "blue-water") Flyfishers take several lines on extra spools with them on the boat each day. Depending on what fish they're after, these

Flyfishers may troll (let the line be pulled behind the boat) instead of casting, or they might just drop the heaviest line they have and let it sink while the boat sits at anchor. Even though they may be after tuna or marlin, saltwater Flyfishers are often surprised by hooking fish they don't expect.

Different Lines For Different Fishing

As you can see, whether you fish in a lake, a river, or in salt water, you will probably be fishing most often with a line that floats. Most people choose to fish with their floating line whenever they can. It's easier to cast and easier to see the line and the fly.

Blair

I prefer a floating line because it's on top of the water where I can see it.

Floating Lines

Like Blair, most people find that when the end of their line is under water, it's harder to tell when a fish bites. There are other reasons for preferring a floating line, though.

Samantha prefers a floating line because the heavier section on the front end of a sink-tip line changes the way it casts.

Samantha

I prefer a floating line over a sink-tip because the river that I fish is not very deep. I also don't use sink-tip lines because it's more work to cast them.

Still, Sam knows all too well that when you have to fish deeper than you can get with a floating line and split-shot (lead weight), a sink-tip line is called for. That is often the case when fishing for salmon, as Sam does.

Alex

Mostly I use floating lines, but in Alaska I had to use a sink-tip line because the salmon were on the bottom. I'm still learning how to manage sink-tips.

As I get to fish more and more places, I'll probably have more occasions to use them.

Alyssa

I've used both floating and sink-tip lines. They both have their uses for different fish and different fishing conditions. I really don't prefer one over the other.

A floating line is easier to cast and easier to see, but sometimes you just need to fish deeper. So, how do you know what kind of sink-tip line to get?

Sink-tip Lines

Sink-tip (or sinking-tip) fly lines have a front section that sinks, while the backend floats. Manufacturers can make the tip of a line sink slowly, fairly fast, or really, really fast. This is called the sink rate. They also make the sinking part in various lengths. You guessed it, that's called the sink length. They put the sink rate and sink length together in lots of different combinations. It can get a bit confusing. Since most people can't afford to buy a separate sink-tip line for each fishing situation, they try to buy one that is versatile instead. That's usually a line with about a ten or twelve-foot-long sink-tip with what is called an intermediate (or medium) sink rate.

A floating line is easier to cast and see.

Although not perfect, it will work fine in lakes, rivers, the surf, and sometimes even in the ocean.

The Right Reel

Now, let's go back to your reel for a minute. No matter whether you use a floating or a sink-tip line, your reel needs to be the correct size to hold your fly line. You don't need a different reel for each fly line you use, but you will need to have more than one spool for your reel. You will probably want to be able to fish with both floating and sink-tip lines someday, so be sure you can buy an extra spool for the reel you choose.

Buy your floating line first. Then, when you decide to buy a sink-tip line, take your reel into the store with you, so you'll be sure to get a matching spool. Don't forget to tell the salesperson which hand you use for winding.

You'll want to be able to remove and replace these spools easily and quickly, so try changing the spools in the store before you buy a reel. Avoid reels with bars that stand up along the reel base or that have a ledge on top of the reel base. Designs like this make changing spools a real pain.

If you're fishing in salt water, your reel has to withstand erosion that could ruin it. It should be made of aluminum, not steel, and it needs to have a special anodized finish. Many quality reels have this finish, whether they're used for fresh water or salt water. Ask about it when you buy your reel.

Remember that you're going to need more drag to slow down a big fish. Some reels also have what's called an "exposed rim." Such a reel enables you to press the palm of your hand flat up underneath the spool when it's turning to provide even more drag. They're recommended for large fish.

Samantha

I was playing a fifteen-pound chum salmon when I first learned to palm the reel. The spool was going around really fast as the fish took off, and the winding knob really hurt when it hit my knuckles. Pudge reached over and showed me how to flatten my hand underneath the reel to slow down the turns of the spool. It worked, and I finally got my fish in.

Sam's lesson is a good one. A strong drag and an exposed rim are essential for fighting big fish.

A strong drag and an exposed rim for palming are essential.

Alex had a somewhat different experience as she was playing a fish. When I reminded her to press the palm of her hand up against the base of the reel to help slow her salmon down, we realized that her rented reel didn't have an exposed rim and was not designed for palming. It took a little longer than expected to get her fish in because she couldn't palm her reel, but she managed.

Blair

Be careful when you have a fish on the line. Your hands should be properly placed on the reel or on the wind-knob. I learned from that mistake. You need the right kind of reel for big fish.

As you can see, it's important to match up your gear with the water you're planning to fish and the fish you're targeting.

Whether you're fishing in a lake, a river, or in salt water, you should also get in the habit of watching and listening to other anglers, as well as asking lots of questions. Are the fish in different places at different times of the year? How does the high water after a rain affect the fishing? What kind of flies are people using?

The answers to questions such as these will be helpful in making it all come together: the water, the fish, and the right gear. The more you learn, the better fly fisher you're going to be.

Alex

There's always something new to learn in fly fishing. It may be a species of fish, some different types of flies, or different kinds of water with new challenges. It's part of what makes fly fishing such a great sport.

As Alex says, there's always something new to learn, and before you can go fly fishing anywhere-lakes, rivers, or salt water-there are other things you must know how to do. From this chapter and the previous one, you know the basics of choosing your fly rod, fly reel, and fly line. Now it's time to learn how to cast.

CHAPTER 7

MAKING LOOPS: CASTING A FLY ROD

Okay, so fly-fishing's a lot of fun. It's different from other kinds of fishing, and there are several ways you might get started. Our river girls-Samantha, Alex, Blair, and Alyssa-all got their feet wet in different ways. No matter how they began, though, all of them learned three basic things: how to cast the rod, what fly to use, and how to actually fish with a fly rod.

In this chapter, we'll cover casting the fly rod. Taking lessons from someone is by far the best way to learn to cast, but what we talk about here will help you know what the lessons will be like and will give you something to refer to after your lessons are over.

Two fundamental casts will get you started. One is the overhead cast and the other is the roll cast.

THE OVERHEAD CAST

Here's how your casting lessons will work, at a glance. Your instructor will have taught you how to attach the reel to the rod and how to string up the rod. She will probably have you begin the lesson without any fly line out the end of your rod. As you get comfortable with the movements required, then you'll pull some line out.

When it's time to do that, you'll slide the line through the guides or eyes that are fixed along the length of the rod. Some of your line will extend out from the rod tip and lie on the ground waiting for you to start casting. A piece of clear, nylon monofilament line called a leader will be tied to the end of the fly line. (Leaders are discussed in the next chapter.) A bright piece of yarn will be tied to the end of the leader, in place of a fly.

You'll grip the rod with four fingers wrapped around the cork handle and your thumb on top of it. Most people hold the rod in the hand that they write with. We call that your rod hand. Your other hand is called your line hand, because it holds the line while you cast and fish.

Your instructor may hold a hand over yours as you try to cast.

There's also a correct way to stand when you're casting. Your feet will be about six inches apart. The foot that's on the opposite side of your rod hand should be just a little in front. This helps you balance your body as you cast.

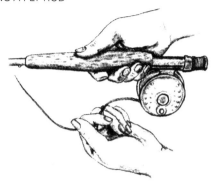

When your instructor demonstrates the basic overhead cast, watch closely as her arm and rod move back and forth.

Those movements are the key to casting, and you'll see the line sail out behind and in front of her, making nice, candy-cane loops at either end.

Then you'll get to try it. At first, your instructor will probably hold a hand over yours as you try casting. This will help direct your hand where it should go and help you understand how it feels to make the rod work.

～

Fly casting is a kind of wizardry. It's a special sort of magic that makes the line go out. As your instructor will show you, the magic happens from two things. First, there are certain "magic" places where your thumb must make your hand and the rod stop. Second, there's a certain "magic" rhythm for making the rod go back and forth. When you get both the stops and the rhythm just right, your line will make candy canes just like your instructor's.

Just so you'll have it written down to refer to as you practice after your lessons, here's how your instructor might help you to find those magic stops and get that magic rhythm.

Find the Magic Stops
- Step 1: Put on a baseball cap. (You'll see why in a minute.) Don't pull out any line yet; practice first just with the rod. Later in the steps, you'll get to try casting with the line out.
- Step 2: With your arm slightly out from the side of your body and with your elbow bent, point your thumb and the rod tip toward the ground in front of you.
- Step 3: Swoop (that means put some "umph" into it) your hand and rod up to a spot just behind your ear and stop it there. Your thumb should be pointed straight up to the sky when your hand stops. That keeps your wrist from bending. Straight wrists help make the line go out. Be sure to move your rod quickly and stop abruptly. In fly casting, the motion you've just made is called the "backcast."

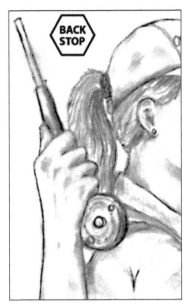

- Step 4: Now, swoop your hand and rod forward to a spot where you can see it just at the end of the bill of your baseball cap. Stop your "front cast" there. (See why you needed the baseball cap? It gives you a reference point for where to stop the forward movement of the rod.)
- Step 5: Now, swoop your hand and rod back and forth between these two spots, stopping abruptly each time. Keep your wrist straight each time. Repeat this motion several times until your brain remembers exactly where the spots are.

The spot behind your ear and the spot at the end of the bill on your baseball cap are the magic stops. Those are the two places where the rod must stop during your cast. The art of making these two stops in these two particular places (along with the magic rhythm that comes next) creates the magic of casting a fly rod. (No stops, no magic. That's one of the secrets the river woman taught our original river girl.)

Get the Magic Rhythm

- Step 6: Now let's add the rhythm of casting. (You still shouldn't have any line out while you practice this.) Your hand and rod have to go back and forth between the magic stops in a regular tempo. While they're learning, almost everybody gets the rhythm by saying some words to help get the timing right. Your instructor will probably have some suggestions for you.

- Step 7: Use the rhythm words your instructor suggests or try saying, "back, stop, and wait" and "forward, stop, and wait," as you move your hand between those magic stops. Obviously, your hand will be at the stop behind your ear as you finish saying "back, stop, and wait," and you'll see it just at the end of the bill of your cap when you finish saying, "forward, stop, and wait." While you're practicing, one complete back-and-forward process should take about three seconds. Be sure your thumb and your rod are actually stopped and waiting, not moving, when you say "wait." The "wait" is really important. If you don't wait, the line will get tangled because it won't have time to straighten out of its candy-cane loop.
- Step 8: Okay, now string up your rod, pull about fifteen feet of fly line out from the tip, and try casting with a fly line. (Always wear glasses or sunglasses to protect your eyes when you're casting.) Just lay the line on the ground in front of you and follow the steps below. You should have a small piece of bright yarn tied on the end of your leader, so you can see where the line is going as you cast.
- Step 9: Point your rod tip toward the ground in front of you. With your line hand, pull enough line off the reel so that you can hold the line comfortably in front of you, about waist high. Your line hand should hold the line firmly and stay in that position as you cast. (Unlike spin-casting, you do not hold the line under the fingers of your rod hand as you cast.)

- Step 10: Start your backcast by swooping your hand and rod back to the spot behind your ear. Stop. Wait. Then swoop forward to the spot at the end of your baseball cap. Stop. Wait. Be sure to say the rhythm words and keep your thumb pointing up toward the sky as you go back and forth between the stops. Remember to keep your wrist straight to make the line go out. Repeat the movements to keep the line moving back and forth.

Soon you should begin to feel when the line has straightened out on your backcast and is ready to go forward. You'll also develop the feeling on the front cast when the line is ready to go back, but during the front cast, you'll be able to see the line straightening out, too. If you hear a snap or "whoosh" or if your line is getting wound around your rod, your rhythm is too fast. If the line just flops, instead of going out straight, that means one of two things. Either your rhythm is too slow, or you're not keeping your thumb pointed to the sky while you make your stops. If you and a friend can practice together, you can watch each other and give suggestions.

As you practice these motions, you'll have the rod going back and forth lots and lots of times, until your arm learns what it's supposed to do. What you're doing is called "false casting," and the line should not hit the ground behind you or in front of you. When you're ready to stop false casting and take a break, do the next step to finish the cast.

- Step 11: When you're ready to finish your cast, stop your hand and rod at the magic spot just at the end of your baseball cap. When the line begins to drop toward the ground in front of you, follow through on your cast by lowering the tip of your rod toward the ground as the line, leader, and yarn fall.

When you're actually out fishing, you'll usually only false cast a couple of times to get enough line out to reach the fish. Your instructor will help you learn how to let line out as you false cast. When you're fishing, of course, you'll also have a fly attached to your line, so the less you false cast, the less chance the hook will catch in a tree or your cap.

You might be a little worried at first that the line will hit you as you cast, but you'll quickly see that the line is going back and forth to the side of your head, not directly above it. You'll be learning with yarn on the end of your leader instead of a fly, so you don't have to worry about a hook either. Glasses or sunglasses will give you eye protection no matter what you're casting. Always wear them.

With some practice, it won't be long before you'll be throwing those pretty candy cane loops. You'll be casting!

Alex

You can't just throw a fly line out like you can with a spinning rod. You have to do a very different cast. It's fun because you get a rhythm going and let out line a little at a time. I like how beautiful the line looks sailing through the air. Once you get good at it, you'll be so proud you've learned to do something that's not really easy.

Like all fly fishers, Alex prefers the basic overhead cast and uses it most of the time, although she is learning the roll cast and the sidearm cast.

"I realize I'll need to know other casts for the different places I'll be fishing," she says.

<h2 style="text-align:center">THE ROLL CAST</h2>

Sometimes there are bushes or trees behind you on the lake or river, and you'll have trouble using the overhead cast without getting caught up in leaves or branches. In this case, you need a cast where your line doesn't go out in the back. That's the roll cast.

The roll cast takes a little practice, but it isn't difficult to do. Here's how your instructor will probably show it to you.

Hold the line firmly in your line hand.

- Step 1: Pull out about twenty feet of fly line and let it lie on the water or grass in front of you. (A lake is the best place to learn the roll cast, but grass will also work.) Now, slowly pull the rod and the lineup and back until your thumb is next to your shoulder, pointing to the sky.
- Step 2: Now tilt your rod tip back a little bit behind you and also out a little bit away from your body, still keeping your thumb pointed to the sky. Wait until the line stops moving in front of you.
- Step 3: Then quickly poke your thumb and the rod tip up toward the sky about five inches and immediately flip the rod tip forward in a little arc with a quick flick of your wrist. Stop it at the magic front stop right at the end of the bill of your baseball

You'll be throwing those pretty candy-cane loops before long.

cap. That poke toward the sky and the flip of the rod tip will send the line out in front of you.

Did you notice that there is no backcast this time? As you practice with your friend, watch as she does the roll cast and you'll see that the line action all happens in front of her. Now let her watch you do it.

Although it's designed to help you avoid getting your fly caught in the trees, the roll cast can also be used when your arm gets tired. Don't be too worried if your line doesn't go out really straight in the beginning. You have to work on your timing and on making the stop in the front in just the right place. When you do, you'll see your fly line taking your fly right out to the fish.

Alex and Blair had to roll cast a number of times when we were salmon fishing because there were people standing on the bank behind us. They certainly didn't want to risk hooking anyone with their backcast. They could not cast the line out as far as they did when they were using the overhead cast, but it really didn't matter. We could see the salmon swimming right at our feet, just waiting for our flies.

~

Learning to fly cast correctly can be a challenge, but your instructor will help you get past the rough parts. Once you have the basics down, practice whenever you can in the backyard or a nearby park. Practicing your casting will help you get ready to do some actual fishing, but first there are a couple of other things we need to discuss. We'll do that in the next chapters.

The Roll Cast.

The roll cast is designed
to help avoid getting your
fly caught in the trees.

CHAPTER 8
RIGGING UP: KNOTS AND LEADERS

Just as in other sports, such as sailing and climbing, the art of tying knots is important to your success as a Flyfisher. Knots are what enable you to tie on your fly in the proper manner. When you first start out as a fly fisher, there are really only two basic knots you need to know. There are variations on these knots and many other useful knots, some of which require a special tool to tie, so you can expand your knot tying ability as you progress. For now, we'll concentrate just on the basics.

Attaching a fly to the end of your line is a two-step process. You don't tie the fly directly to the end of your fly line, because the fly line is thick and very visible to the fish. Besides, you couldn't do that even if you wanted to, because the fly line is too fat to go through the eye of your hook. Instead, you use a special piece of line to make the connection. It's called a "leader." It does exactly what you would expect; it "leads" from the end of your fly line out to the fly. When you cast, you're actually casting a fly line, a leader, and a fly.

Leaders are made of monofilament line-a clear strand of nylon like the kind you may have used on a spinning rod. You might also have used monofilament to string beads. The leader helps the fly to land correctly when you cast and also keeps the fish from seeing the fly line.

Leaders are generally six to nine feet in length. When you're beginning, we recommend that you use a six-and-a-half-foot or seven-and-a-half-foot leader. They're easy to cast and keep your fly line far enough away from the fly so that the fish don't see it. Later, you may need to use shorter or longer leaders.

Leaders taper down from a thicker diameter to a smaller thickness that is still strong enough to catch the fish you're after. Flyfishers call the thicker part of the leader the "butt" section. That's the end attached to the fly line. The thinner, front section is called the "tippet." That's the end to which you'll attach the fly.

First, we'll learn how to attach the leader to the fly line, and then we'll learn the two primary knots you'll need: the improved clinch knot-for tying a fly to the leader-and the surgeon's knot-for tying pieces of leader together. Learning to tie knots is a part of fly fishing that you should get some help with from your

The art of tying knots is important to your success as a flyfisher.

instructor or your folks. With a bit of practice, you'll soon be: able to do try everything by yourself. You'll notice that our illustrations use a ring, rather than a fly with a hook. That's a good way to practice knot tying.

ATTACHING THE LEADER TO THE FLY LINE

Earlier in the book, we said that the salesperson at the store where you purchase your equipment will usually load the fly line onto the reel for you. The next step is to attach a leader to the fly line. The salesperson will attach a small, permanent loop of heavy monofilament on the end of the fly line and then help you choose the right size leader to connect to it. Like rods and line, a leader should be matched to the size of the fish you intend to catch.

The leaders you buy should already have a loop on the butt section. Most manufacturers do that for you, but you should check. To attach the leader to your fly line, you'll be putting that loop together with the loop on the end of the fly line using what is known as the loop-to-loop connection. This isn't really a knot, but here's how it works.

Connecting the two loops is easy. Just put the loop on the end of your fly line through the loop on the end of your leader. Then take the tippet (the skinny end of your leader) and put it through the loop on the end of your fly line. Pull the tippet, while holding the fly line, to make a tight, square-looking knot, like the one in the illustration. You can take the leader off by simply pushing the loops together to loosen them and then reversing the process.

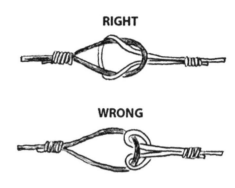

RIGHT

WRONG

TYING ON THE FLY

The knot most commonly used to tie on a fly is called the improved clinch knot. If you've fished with a spinning rod in the past, you may have used this knot to tie on your lure. Here it is.

To attach the leader to the fly line, you'll use a loop-to-loop connection.

Step 1   **Step 2**

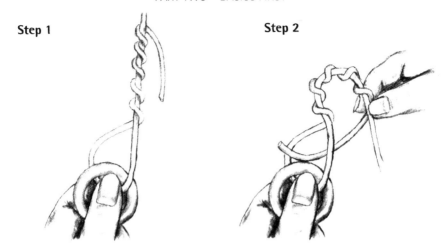

Improved Clinch Knot

- Step 1: Put six inches of tippet through the eye of the hook. Lay this short piece of monofilament alongside the long section. Hold the hook by the eye and wrap the short piece loosely around the long section five times with the wraps going over the top and away from you.
- Step 2: Take the end of the short piece (the one you've been wrapping with) and poke it back towards yourself through the hole above the hook eye that formed when you started to make the wraps. Notice that poking it through the hole forms another loop.
- Step 3: Now poke the end of the short piece back through the loop that you just formed in Step 2.

Step 3   **Step 4**

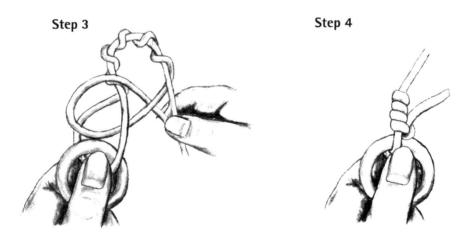

Spit lubricates the tippet while you're tightening the knot.

- Step 4: Now put the line in your mouth to put spit on it. That lubricates the tippet while you're tightening the knot. While holding the end of the short piece with your teeth, pull the fly and the long end of the leader in opposite directions. This will tighten the knot. You can use your fingers to help guide the knot, so it snugs up against the eye of the hook. Before you clip the end that is sticking out to make the knot neat, hold the fly and pull on the leader to make sure the knot is set.

If you're fishing for large fish or fishing in salt water, you'll probably see or hear about some stronger knots you should learn to tie. Have your instructor or your folks show them to you.

You can buy spools of tippet material where you buy leaders.

TYING LEADER SECTIONS TOGETHER

As you fish throughout the day, you're likely to change flies several times to find the best one and to keep the fish interested. Whenever you do that, you use up some of the skinny end of your leader. After a few fly changes you'll find that the leader is shorter, and the tippet is fatter.

You don't want to have to take off what's left of your leader and throw it away, because replacing the whole leader all the time can get quite expensive. You'll want to learn a knot that you can use just to tie more skinny tippet on to the end of the leader. You can buy spools of tippet material where you buy your leaders. Later in the chapter we'll tell you how to make sure you buy the right size for your leader.

An easy knot to use for tying more tippet on the end of your leader is called the surgeon's knot-and you don't have to be a doctor to use it. Here it is, with illustrations of each step.

Surgeon's Knot

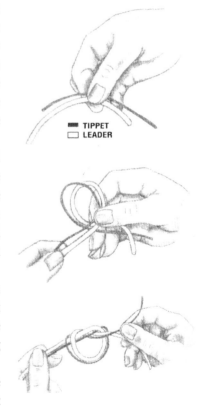

TIPPET
LEADER

- Step 1: Cut off about eighteen inches of the tippet from its spool. (How much you cut off depends on how much you've used up. Cut enough to make the leader as long as it was when it was new.) Put the new tippet material side-by-side with the end of the remaining leader, with the two lines pointing in opposite directions. Have them overlap about six or seven inches.
- Step 2: Pick up the two lines, with one end of the overlapped lines in one hand and the other end in your other hand. You'll have a short end and a long end of line in each hand. Now make an overhand knot and pull the loose pair of short and long ends through the loop. Don't pull the loop tight yet.
- Step 3: Holding a short and a long line in each hand, put the knot in your mouth and put some spit on it to make the monofilament slide easier. Now pull on each set of short and long ends to tighten the knot.
- Step 4: Clip the two short ends of the line sticking out of the knot to make a neat knot that won't get hung up on weeds and rocks as you fish.

For larger fish, it's important to use a double or triple surgeon's knot.

Many people use what it known as a double surgeon's knot or even a triple surgeon's knot by repeating the overhand knot in Step 2 one or two more times before tightening the knot. The basic surgeon's knot will hold small fish, but when you fish for average-size or larger fish, it's smart to increase the knot's strength by using a double or triple surgeon's knot.

With the surgeon's knot, you can tie on more tippet any time you need it. Of course, you'll need to have a spool of the right size tippet in your vest so that you can add it to your leader when you need to.

It's easy to know which size of tippet material to buy. Just look on the package of the leader you bought, and it will tell you what pound-test the butt section of the leader is and what pound-test the tippet section is. It also gives a number with an "X" beside it. The X-number indicates the diameter of the leader at the skinny end. There's a whole system for using these numbers to show the leader diameter, which you'll learn as you go along. To start with, you just need to match the X-number of the tippet spool you buy with the X-number of your original leader.

After you become a more experienced Flyfisher, you might even want to learn to tie your own leaders, from butt section to tippet. That's what happened to Sam. She had someone tie on both her leader and her fly when she first started fly-fishing. That is what most young people do. Soon, though, she proceeded to use the commercially made leaders you buy in the store and learned how to tie on her own tippet material and fly.

Then, Sam asked me if I'd teach her how to tie the knots that enable a fly fisher to create her own leaders. She practiced and practiced, even sitting in on some of the knot tying lessons I held for my fly fishing clients. Her confidence improved at every turn. Now she doesn't have to buy leaders anymore; she knows how to tie her own, using a special knot-tying tool I gave her and different spools of leader material.

～

There's always something new to learn in the sport of fly fishing. Whether you're starting to tie your own leaders or a new knot, using a new casting technique, or exploring a new river, it's always interesting and exciting. That's why so many fly fishers have enjoyed being on the water their entire lives. We're glad you're joining them.

As a beginner, there's one more thing you need to learn about before you're ready to go fly fishing, and that's the flies we use. We'll cover that in the next chapter.

CHAPTER 9

FOOLING FISH WITH FUR AND FEATHERS: THE FLYS

Trying to duplicate what the fish were eating was the very first way people actually fly-fished. They watched fish grabbing bugs off the surface of the water and gobbling up smaller fish. When they tried to capture and use live insects, they found that getting a bug to stay on a hook didn't work very well. Before long, they began to imitate insects and small fish, using materials such as fur, hair, and feathers. They figured that if they could trick the fish into thinking their fake was the real thing, they could catch them. It worked, and fly fishing was born.

Beginning fly fishers find out fast that the flies they use are crucial to success. You can have the highest quality, most expensive equipment on the market, but if you don't choose the right fly, you don't catch fish. Just as people sometimes prefer fried chicken over hamburgers, fish are interested in certain foods at different times. Still, their food preferences relate to the kinds of food most available in their world. The challenge for fly fishers is to use flies that imitate those food sources closely enough to fool fish. Which fly you choose will depend, first of all, on whether you're fishing in fresh water or salt water.

FRESHWATER FLIES

A typical beginning fly fishing class includes a lesson about flies. You'll learn that fly fishers create flies in many different sizes and shapes to imitate nearly anything that fish eat. In fresh water, fish feed mainly on insects that live in the water, small bait fish, leeches (icky, but true), snails, frogs, and critters that fall in the water, especially insects such as ants, grasshoppers, and beetles. If they happen to live where the eggs of other fish are plentiful, they'll eat those, too.

When you learn about freshwater flies, this is how your lesson might go. Your instructor sets three flies on the table on a piece of white paper. Each one has a label. There's a tiny, fuzzy, tan-colored fly with a bushy little upright wing on

If you don't choose the right fly, you don't catch fish.

top. That one is labeled "Dry Fly." Next, there's one that's about the same size that doesn't have the bushy wing. Its body is usually fatter in the front than it is in the back. It's labeled "Nymph." The third fly is both larger and longer than the other two and quite furry. It's called a "Streamer."

Alex

I've fished with lots of different flies. Every place we fish, we have to use some unique ones. I love learning about them. They have great names, like Woolly Bugger.

There you have the three basic kinds of freshwater flies-dry flies, nymphs, and streamers. They imitate the foods that fish eat the most: bugs on top of the water, bugs underneath the water, and bait fish or leeches. You guessed it, the one with the bushy wing, the dry fly, imitates bugs that can fly. The nymph, the small one without the bushy wing, is meant to look like a bug when it's living underwater. The long one that also doesn't have bushy, upright wings, the streamer, imitates something that lives underwater and can't fly away, it's meant to look like a bait fish or a leech.

Dry Flies

Which one of the flies do you think will float on the water the best? If you suspect that the fuzzy fly with the bushy wing would float better than the other two, you're right. Dry flies are designed to float. The materials they're made of keep them from sinking. A fly fisher can distinguish them by the way they're tied, with bushy hair or "hackle" sticking out from the hook all the way around.

Alyssa

I like dry-fly fishing the best, because the flies are easy to see floating on the water. Besides, you can also see the fish grab your fly. Now that's exciting!

The study of bugs, entomology, tells us that the insects that are the fish's favorites hatch from eggs that are laid in the water. When the eggs of some of these insects, such as caddisflies, hatch, the first life stage of the bug looks sort of like tiny worms. These are called larvae. Over a period of several months, the larvae take on a more buggy shape, with obvious legs and wings, and are then called pupae. They look more like real bugs. This is when they get ready to swim to the surface and emerge as adults.

Other insects, such as mayflies, hatch from their eggs as nymphs and live in that form for about a year until they swim to the shore and crawl out or swim to the surface of the water, where they pop out of their shells, unfurl their wings, and fly away.

Flyfishers know that fish eat aquatic bugs in all their life stages. Fish usually prefer the larger underwater forms and the adults with wings, because they make a bigger meal. The flies that imitate the immature forms-larvae, pupae, and nymphs-are generally all referred to as "nymphs." Lots of different dry flies are used to imitate adult bugs with wings.

Have you ever watched bugs flying around and landing on a river or lake? Have you ever seen the rings that appear on the surface of a quiet lake on a lazy summer evening? Those rings mean the fish are eating bugs on or near the surface. Sometimes they are bugs that are swimming up and emerging. Other times they are adult insects that are laying eggs in the water to start the whole life cycle over again.

$\sim$

Fish don't always eat the same kind of bug, of course. They like to eat different kinds of bugs, just the way you like different kinds of pizza. You certainly know the difference between a pepperoni pizza and a vegetarian pizza; the fish also know which kind of bug they prefer at different times. Often, they prefer the insect that is most abundant or easiest to catch.

The three kinds of bugs that are proven fish favorites are the caddisfly, the mayfly, and the stonefly. Try to identify the adults of these three kinds of insects each time you go fishing. Here are some tips on how to do it. When it is resting, the caddisfly folds its wings together over its back to look like a pair of hands folded in prayer or a tiny tent. A mayfly is a slender bug with a long, forked, up-thrusting tail and lovely, oval wings that also sweep upwards into the air. Caddis and mayflies are found pretty much everywhere, in rivers and lakes, in warm water and cold water.

Last, but not least, the third bug looks like a long, fat stick with legs. From the picture you can see that it has wings, but they're folded flat on top of its body. Those bugs are called stoneflies. Some of them grow up to be three or four inches long, and they make a big meal for a fish, sort of like a steak and baked potato dinner for us. Stoneflies are found mainly in rivers. As adults, they spend a lot of time resting in the bushes with their wings flattened out. Look along the riverbank and you can often find the shucks they leave behind when they change from being nymphs to being adults with wings.

Go to a nearby creek or lake and look around to see if you can spot any of the three great fish-getters. Practice identifying them, so you can choose flies that imitate the bugs on the water.

When you go fishing, you should always look into the air and at bushes near the water to see which kind of bug is around. When you figure that out, you'll have a good idea of which fly to use. Of course, there are many other flies that imitate each kind of bug; you'll learn them as you get more experience. The three pictured on the previous page will serve you well for starters.

Nymphs

As you've learned, immature aquatic insects live under the surface of the river or lake before they emerge as adults. Lift a rock out of the river and turn it over to see them.

Remember that although these immature forms have many scientific names-larva, pupa, nymph-the imitations of them are all called "nymphs" by fly fishers.

There's one nymph that's such a good imitation of lots of different insects that it's known as the "universal nymph." The name of this fly is the Gold-ribbed Hare's Ear. Like many flies, it has a silly name. It got its name because it has gold ribbing and it's tied mainly with rabbit fur. You can use it any time you go fishing in lakes or rivers, even when you see swarms of bugs on the surface of the water or flying around.

Two other flies that are good, general purpose nymphs are called the Pheasant Tail (take a guess why), which is pictured earlier in the chapter, and the Zug Bug (named for its creator, Christopher Zug). You can see that all of these flies are kind of flat in the back and fatter in the front. That's the way the real underwater insects look.

Just from this discussion, you can figure out that you would use the little dry flies when there are lots of bug in the air and on the surface of the water where the fish can grab them. You would use nymphs beneath the water's surface when the winged bugs aren't around.

Fish don't stop feeding just because there are no bugs in the air. Nope, they just switch to eating under the water. Just because you can't see the fish actually eating the nymphs, don't get fooled into thinking you have to stop fishing.

Dry Flies and the Insects They Imitate

Here are pictures of the freshwater fish's three favorite bugs and a popular dry fly that imitates the ault of each kind of bug. An Elk Hair Caddis imitates a real Caddisfly. The one called a Stimulator looks like a stonefly.

Streamers

Like nymphs, streamers can also be used when fish aren't feeding on top of the water. Streamers are meant to imitate things larger than the bugs that fish eat. These include foods like little bait fish, leeches (yucky to us, but yummy to fish), and so on. Depending on what they mimic, streamers can be bright or dark, silvery or dull. Colorful, shiny streamers are sometimes referred to as "attractors."

Just like dry flies and nymphs, streamers come in lots of different colors and shapes, but you can get started with just the two streamers in the pictures below.

The first fly has a soft, fluffy tail and a long body with little hairs sticking up all around it like tiny legs. This is a very, very famous imitation of a leech. It's called a Woolly Bugger. Go ahead, laugh at the

weird name, but in different sizes and colors, this fly catches lots and lots of fish! Just ask Alex.

Woolly Buggers can be used on both rivers and lakes. Some people say that more fish have been caught on Woolly Buggers than all the other flies combined. Black, purple, and olive are considered the best colors to use.

The second great streamer fly has a long, gold body, a swept-back wing that looks like part of a duck feather, and a head of deer hair clipped sort of like a crew cut. It's called a Muddler Minnow. Another funny name.

Samantha

Muddlers are some of the first flies I ever fly-fished with. They're still one of my favorite flies for trout.

This one, too, is a very old and famous fly. Like Sam, many, many fly fishers used this fly when they were starting out. It's considered a reliable standby for trout and even for steelhead, that famous cousin of the rainbow trout that goes to sea and then returns to fresh water.

Muddlers are tied in different sizes. Colors and styles vary according to location. If you look at almost any fly-tying book, you'll see several examples.

~

If you live in a part of the country where bass fishing is popular, your instructor may have one more type of fly to show you, a popper. Poppers are flies that are designed to float on the water. They have large heads made of cork, foam, or clipped deer hair, with trailing feathers or bucktail. When they're jerked along the surface, they actually make a popping sound, and that attracts hungry bass. In small sizes they work well for bluegills, sunfish, and crappie, too.

Wherever you live, your instructor will probably have some examples of different flies so you can see there are many possible sizes, shapes, and colors. Maybe she'll also have a fly-tying book or two that you can page through. It's also fun to take a trip to a nearby fly shop or sporting goods store to look at the variety of flies on display.

The sheer number of different flies can be intimidating. Learning their names can seem impossible. Don't worry; you'll learn as you go. You already know the basic ones for freshwater fly fishing. The following chart will sum it up.

Notice that we recommend size 12 for the dry flies and the nymphs and size 6 or 8 for the streamers. (Fly sizes refer to the size of the hook, and they're backwards; a size12 is smaller than a size 6!) Flies come in lots of sizes, but these are good ones to get started with. You'll learn more about sizes of flies as you go along.

You can use any of these flies-dries, nymphs, or streamers-either on a lake or in a river. Your choice of fly will depend more on what fish food you are trying to imitate or what you see happening (or not happening) on the water than on where you're fishing. Remember, fly fishing is all about trying to fool the fish into thinking that your little Fur-and-feather fake is the real thing.

SALTWATER FLIES

Now let's suppose you live near the salt water or get to travel to the ocean. If you do, you'll hear about different flies than those we've just talked about. Saltwater fly fishers primarily use flies that have been designed to imitate the bait fish that live in the water in coastal areas. They are, technically speaking, streamer patterns, but we think of them separately because of where they're used and what they look like. Your instructor or your folks will show you some examples and help you to learn more.

Because saltwater fly fishing is newer than fly fishing in fresh water and also because there are many more species of fish in

salt water, the flies for this type of fishing are still being developed. It's not as easy to give you a short list of tried-and-true fish catchers for salt water.

Still, most of the people who fly fish in salt water would probably agree that the following flies would be good ones to get you started: Clouser Minnow, Lefty's Deceiver, and Crazy Charlie. Tied in various sizes, colors, and materials, these three flies account for lots and lots of angling success in the salt.

If you start saltwater fly fishing in the surf from the beach, you'll most likely fish with Clouser Minnows. They're extremely versatile flies. Typically tied in white with tan, olive, green, and yellow trim, they have big, sometimes heavy eyeballs that can make them difficult to cast. Your instructor can help you adjust your casting to get these flies out into the water.

BASIC DRY FLIES, NYMPHS, AND STREAMERS		
Dry Flies-Size 12	*Nymphs-Size 12*	*Streamers-Size 6 or 8*
1. Elk Hair Caddis 2. Adams 3. Stimulator	1. Gold-ribbed Hare's Ear 2. Pheasant Tail 3. Zug Bug	1. Woolly Bugger 2. Muddler Minnow

Lefty's Deceiver is named for its designer, a very famous fly fisher named Lefty Kreh. He's probably taught more people to fly fish and to improve their casting than any four or five other top instructors combined. He's also one of the pioneers of saltwater fly fishing. His Deceiver is a "never-leave-home-without it" fly for the salt.

As you look at the Deceiver, you'll notice it's quite a large fly. The eyes are usually pasted onto the sides of the head rather than sticking out like the Clouser's. That's because Deceivers (unless they're intentionally tied small) are most frequently used when fishing from a boat, rather than when fishing from shore. Deceivers tied with green or blue backs are the most popular because those colors imitate the dark backs of most bait fish.

The Crazy Charlie is another great fly. It's used both from the shore and when wading in the shallows (called the "flats"). It is supposed to suggest a small shrimp or crab that the fish might be pursuing. The Charlie has eyes sticking out from the sides of the hook. That's because the eyes of shrimp and crabs protrude from their bodies.

You'll probably start out with one of these three flies, but if not, be sure to ask the name of a fly that someone gives you to use. Write it down so you can remember to use it again, especially if it catches fish!

~

Whether you fish in fresh water or salt, learning about different flies is all part of the fun of fly fishing. Like Sam, you'll probably want to learn to tie your own flies eventually, rather than having to buy them all the time. Once she got started tying flies for her herself, you'll remember that Sam also tied them for some of the clients at her mom's lodge. She knows which flies work on her river, and she's become very good at creating them.

It's time to move on now. You've got the basics on equipment, casting, leaders and knots, and flies, so you're ready for the final step. Let's go next to the basics of how to fish with a fly rod.

When you cast, your line is
held in your line hand.

CHAPTER 10

REELING THEM IN:
FISHING WITH A FLY ROD

W hen you've mastered fly casting well enough to get your line out, you're ready to see what fishing with a fly rod is all about. You already know that it's different from the spin fishing or bait fishing that you may have tried.

Remember, in those types of fishing you're throwing something heavy (a lure or a chunk of bait) out toward the fish, and the line gets pulled along when you sling that weight toward the target.

In fly fishing there's nothing heavy to "throw." Flies weigh hardly anything. Instead, it's the magic stops and rhythm that make the tip of the fly rod zing the weight of the line out toward the fish. Your back-and-forth cast makes that happen.

Okay, so you know how to cast, so you can get your fly out where the fish are. Now what? Just like fly casting, fly fishing is a series of steps.

CASTING AND LINE CONTROL

- Step 1: Using the overhead cast, make two or three false casts to get your line out. Then aim your rod tip at a spot where you think the fish are. (Remember, when you cast, the line is held in your line hand, not your rod hand.)
- Step 2: When you're ready to deliver the fly, stop your hand and rod at the magic spot just at the end of your baseball cap. When the line begins to drop toward the water, follow through on your cast by lowering the tip of your rod toward the water.
- Step 3: As soon as your fly falls on the water, use your line hand to loop the fly line over one or both of the first two fingers of your rod hand and hold it loosely there against the cork handle. With your line hand, take hold of the fly line between your rod hand and the reel, so that you always have control of the line.

Follow through on your cast by lowering the tip of the rod.

Use these three basic steps, whether you're fishing in a river, a lake, or salt water and no matter which kind of fly you're using. What you do after you make your cast and have control of your line, depends on the kind of water you're fishing and the type of fly you're using. Let's take them one at a time.

FLYFISHING IN A RIVER

When you're fishing a river or a stream, your fly is moving downriver with the current. You'll typically cast upstream, putting your fly upriver of the place where you think the fish are, so the fly can drift down naturally to them. The drift of the fly may take it past several good places for fish, so let it drift until it drags or gets close to you before you cast again.

Your job is to help the fly drift without the fly line dragging it and to watch carefully so you'll see the things that indicate a fish is biting.

Getting a Natural Drift

To help the fly drift naturally with the current, just like a real insect, the first thing you'll do after your fly lands on the water is to make one or two little half-moon circles upstream with your rod tip, as shown in the illustration on the next page. This is called "mending" line. It's an important motion that keeps your fly moving along without your line dragging it. It takes some practice, and it helps to get some instruction or watch other fly fishers who use this technique.

94

What you do after you've mended your line depends on whether you're using a dry fly on the surface or a nymph or streamer under the water.

Fishing a Dry Fly in a River

If you're fishing a dry fly, keep your rod tip pointed directly at the fly as it floats along. With the fly line held loosely in the first two fingers of your rod hand, pull in a little bit of line with your line hand (that's called "stripping" line), as the fly drifts closer to you.

Stripping line will help you to keep a fairly straight line between the rod tip and your fly. Lots of slack line on the water makes it hard to hook the fish, but too little slack may cause the line to drag the fly across the surface. You'll soon learn how fast to strip the line.

Your job now is to watch the dry fly carefully as it floats along so you can see the fish come to the surface and grab your fly. When you see a "rise," you'll set the hook. (We'll talk about setting the hook a little later.) Seeing the dry fly on the surface of a river isn't always easy, but you'll get the knack. Polarized sunglasses help a lot.

If you're fishing with a nymph or a streamer, the fly is underwater so you can't see it. You'll do the same things to keep the fly drifting naturally-mending and stripping in line-but you won't be able to see the fish bite.

Loop the fly line over one or both of the first two fingers of your rod hand and hold it loosely there.

With a nymph or streamer, you'll have to either wait to feel the fish bite or, better yet, watch for some jiggle or twitch at the end of your fly line that indicates a bite. Then it's time to set the hook.

Streamers are sometimes cast across the stream or slightly downstream. If you use this technique, you'll strip in line to imitate a bait fish swimming. Because the line is tighter when you fish that way, you'll often feel the fish bite first.

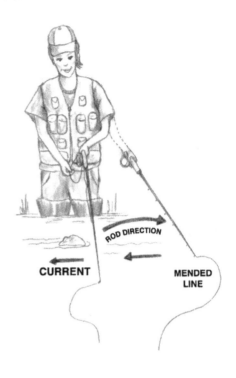

ROD DIRECTION

CURRENT

MENDED LINE

~

Samantha and Blair fish primarily in rivers so they've both had experience with dry fly, nymph, and streamer fishing in moving water. They both find it exciting and interesting. Fly fishing in lakes can be just as much fun.

Keep your rod tip pointed directly at the fly as it floats along.

FLY FISHING IN A LAKE

Fly fishing in a lake is different than in a river, because the water isn't moving. If you want your fly to appear lifelike to the fish (and you do!), then you will have to do something to make that happen. Again, we have different techniques for dry flies and underwater flies. Here are some tips to help you to fish in still water.

Fishing a Dry Fly in a Lake
When you cast a dry fly in a lake, you 'll often aim your rod tip and put your fly near where you see a ring or swirl on the surface. Or you may even aim for a fish you see jumping out of the water after a bug.

It's often a good idea to cast a short distance away from where you saw the ring or swirl. Fish in a lake are always on the move, looking for food. Unless there is lots of food in one place, they may be several feet away from the ring before you get your cast out. Sometimes you can even tell which way they're moving by watching carefully.

After your dry fly lands on the water, the fish may rise to it right away or in a few seconds. If you don't get a rise, your fly will just continue to sit there until you do something or until it gets waterlogged and sinks. There are two things you might do:

- You can try to make the fly look like a bug that is flitting across the water, trying to escape or laying eggs. If you chose this option, you'll need to do short strips of line or jiggle your rod tip to give the fly some lifelike movement. When the fly gets close to you, lift the fly off the water and cast again.
- If you see another ring and think you know where the fish is heading, you can lift the fly off the water and cast again.

All the time the fly is on the water, watch it carefully. If it disappears in a swirl, set the hook.

Fishing a Nymph or Streamer in a Lake
When you cast a nymph or a streamer in a lake, it will sink, because those kinds of flies are meant to imitate fish food that lives underwater. To make the fly imitate the action of underwater insects and bait fish, you'll have to provide movement.

You should experiment to find the depth where the fish are. You can vary how deep you're fishing by waiting before starting your retrieve. On the first cast, you might wait just a couple of seconds. On the next cast, you might count out ten seconds before starting to strip line in, and so on.

Here are some things you might do on the retrieve:

After your dry fly lands on the water, the fish may rise to it right away.

- After the fly drops to the depth you want, start to do short strips of your line with a pause in between to make your fly look like a bug or a leech or a little fish that is swimming towards the surface of the lake.
- After the fly drops to the depth you want, give it an occasional jiggle with the rod tip to see if the fish are interested. Or try a short strip of line followed by a longer wait, letting the fly sink back down. Repeat this several times, and if nothing happens, retrieve the fly and cast again. After your dry fly lands on the water, the fish may rise to it right away.
- If you're fishing from a canoe, boat, or float tube, you can trail the fly out behind you as your boat or float tube moves. That's called "trolling."

FLYFISHING IN SALT WATER

Fly fishing in salt water usually means fishing the surf from the beach or fishing in the shallow flats farther out by wading or casting from a boat.

Fishing in the Surf

Fly fishing the surf isn't really like either river or lake fishing, except that you'll be fishing under the surface of the water with flies that are similar to freshwater streamers. Here are a couple of tips for surf fishing:

When you're fishing from the beach or shore, the water will be moving your fly. Because you're casting out into waves that are coming toward the beach, those waves will usually be moving your fly toward you. So, you might do the following:

- Position your body slightly sideways to the beach so that your fly comes in at an angle to the beach instead of straight in.
- Strip the line to bring your fly in, rather than just letting it sit in the waves, so it will be moving in the water, not just with the water, like a real bait fish.

Fishing the Flats

When you're fishing farther out in the saltwater, you could be wading in shallow water called flats or "parked" in the boat and casting to schools of fish. You could also be trolling your fly behind the boat. If you're wading or casting from the boat, you'll have to strip the fly in some way to give it lifelike movement. If you're trolling, The boat will be moving the fly for you. Experiment and follow the advice of the people you're fishing with to know what type of action works best for the fish you're after.

SETTING THE HOOK AND PLAYING THE FISH

Okay, now you've got an idea of some of the differences in fly fishing rivers, lakes, and saltwater. So, let's get back to the question of how to hook up with the fish that's going after your fly.

Getting the hook stuck solidly in the mouth of a biting fish is known as "setting the hook." If you've fished with a spinning or bait rod, you're probably already familiar with the term. Here are the steps for accomplishing it with a fly rod.

Setting the Hook

- Step 1: When a fish bites, you may either feel it, see your line move, or see a splash where your dry fly was floating. Immediately set the hook. Here's how to do that:
- Tighten the fingers of your rod hand on the fly line and the rod handle and raise the rod tip quickly (but not too hard) to set the hook securely in the fish's mouth. This technique is the best for fishing in freshwater rivers and lakes.

Raise the rod tip quickly
to set the hook.

- In salt water, tighten your fingers on the line and rod handle and move the rod tip sharply out to the side to set the hook. Saltwater fish swim so much faster than freshwater fish that experienced saltwater fly fishers recommend this technique to get better hook-ups.

Okay, you've got 'im! Now what?

Playing the Fish

- Step 2: As The fish swims off, keep your rod tip high (or off to the side if you're in salt water) and let the excess line between your line hand and the reel slide out through your fingers. Don't let go of the line completely, because slack line lets the fish shake the hook loose. But don't hold the line too tightly either, because it will break off if you do. If the fish takes all the excess line and starts pulling line off the reel, let go of the line. Don't hold it with either hand. The line should go straight from the reel to the fish. Get ready to reel, but be sure not to hold onto the wind-knob of the reel while the fish is running. As we've said before, that's a good way to get some very banged-up knuckles.
- Step 3: Control the fish by letting it pull line out when it's running and then reeling or stripping line back in when the fish rests or when there's some slack in the line. If you're playing a large fish strictly with the reel, let the reel's drag control the fish. Palming the reel can also help. Eventually, the fish will get tired and you can "land" it.

- Step 4: When the fish gets close to you and is too tired to fight anymore, raise your rod up and tip it behind you to bring the fish in. That way, if the fish does make another run, your rod is in position to help you control it. Be sure to keep your fish in the water when landing it, if you plan to release it. Practice catch-and-release correctly so your fish can be released unharmed. (Catch-and-release steps are described in Chapter 14.)

Hooking up and playing a fish takes practice, and you'll probably lose some fish when you're beginning. Ask the people you're fishing with to help you the first few times you do it. If you've already been fishing with a spinning or a bait rod, you have a pretty good idea of how important it is to play a fish correctly. Your mom or day may have already hooked a fish and then given the rod to you, so that you could bring the fish in. While you did that, I'll bet they gave you lots of good coaching.

In most fly fishing classes, the instructor will also give you some good coaching, too. She may ask you to hold the rod while she pretends to be a fish and demonstrates how each of the steps for setting the hook and landing the fish work. Then she will probably have you and the other students take turns playing the part of the fish and playing the angler so you can practice landing a fish with a fly rod. When everyone can remember what to do, you're ready to go fly fishing.

Then the fun will start. Just listen to what Alex has to say about it.

Alex

Anyone can pick up a spinning rod and be fishing in no time, but it's harder to get the hang of fly fishing. That takes more concentration. I quickly came to realize that fly fishing was much more fun, though, as I began catching fish with a fly rod. It's a real "rush" to get in close with the fish when I'm wading. The anticipation of waiting for a fish to bite is very exciting!

When the fish gets close, raise your rod tip to bring it in.

PART THREE
Other Essentials

Hip boots keep you
from wading too deep.

CHAPTER 11

WHAT EVER WILL I WEAR? OUTERWEAR, UNDERWEAR, WADERS, AND MORE

The essential gear for fly fishing is, of course, a fly rod, a fly reel, a fly line, a leader, and a fly. Without them you can't fish.

However, there's other equipment for fly fishing that you'll probably be needing sooner or later, particularly as you begin wading in the water. Those things are chesthigh waders, wading boots, and a fly fishing vest.

As you gear up, you'll also begin thinking of what to wear under those waders to keep you warm and what to wear over them to keep you dry (and also warm). We'll take these one at a time.

WADERS

Let's start with waders. It you're already a fisher-girl, you may very well have a pair of hip boots that you wear when you go fishing. Hip boots are okay, if they have felt soles. If they have rubber soles, you can slip easily and fall in the water. Hip boots have the advantage of being easy to put on and take off. They will also keep you from wading too deep (but you shouldn't be wading even as deep as you can with them!).

You may have already discovered that hip boots also have disadvantages. Because they only come to the tops of your legs, you're apt to get cold. They're better for warmer fishing conditions. Also, the gap between your rain coat and the tops of your hip boots means that you're liable to have a wet "behind" when it rains.

Finally, hip boots may be too wide for your feet, causing them to slip around inside the boot. That can result in a fall. You can buy stocking-foot hippers and wading boots (more on this later) or put insoles in regular hip boots to help this problem. Just don't forget that you need felt soles!

Flyfishers usually do more wading than spin or bait fishers do, and they often find themselves unhappy with hip boots. Such was the case with Samantha.

At a young age Sam was already tired of the problems with hip boots and asked repeatedly for some chest-high waders like everyone else. Sam, her mom, and I sat down one evening to have a long discussion about waders. I had an old pair that I was considering giving to Sam. While they were still a little too large for her, they could be rolled down at the waist so Sam could wear them. Claire was worried that her already too brave daughter might wade in farther than was safe, once she didn't have to worry about the water coming over the tops of her hip boots.

I told Sam I'd give her the waders only if her mom and I could be sure she was going to be safe wearing them. She promised that if she were allowed to have the waders, she would not wade in any water that was above her calves. Her mom accepted her promise, and Sam got the waders. She kept her promise, too. Now she felt like a real fly fisher.

Chest-high Waders

Just like Sam, most fly fishers do prefer chest-high waders. The most popular waders are made of either neoprene (the material used in scuba diving suits) or a lighter, more breathable fabric that has neoprene feet. Each type has advantages and disadvantages. Take a look at the chart below and decide which is the best for you.

Left: neoprene waders are warm, and there's more selection for young people. Right: Breathable waders are lighter and easier to pack, but there are not as many models for young people.

COMPARING CHEST-HIGH WADERS		
Type of Wader	*Advantages*	*Disadvantages*
Neoprene	• warmer in cold weather • less expensive • more selection for young people	• can get too hot in warm weather or when hiking • heavier, bulkier • harder to get a good fit
Breathable fabric	• cooler in warm weather • lighter weight • easier to pack when traveling • may have a more boxy shape for easier fit	• no warmth in cold weather • more expensive • not as many models for young people

Both types of chest-high waders are durable, and both are fairly easy to care for. The choice usually comes down to warmth, price, and fit.

As yet, few companies manufacture very much in the way of fly fishing gear for young people. That is changing, however, as more and more girls like you and boys your age get started in the sport.

Blair

I hadn't ever worn waders before I fished in Alaska, but I really liked wearing them when I was fishing. I was warm and dry.

When you're ready to shop for waders, you'll probably start by visiting your local fly fishing shop or sporting goods store. Fly fishing shops are more likely to have or be able to order waders for young people. Take the time to try things on with the clothes and socks you'll be wearing on the river. Be sure to compare prices and give lots of thought to whether you'll be doing most of your fishing in hot or cold weather.

Catalogs such as Cabela's may also have waders for young people. Be sure to check them out. (Remember to use Appendix 1: Shopping Guide for Gearing Up when you go to the store or order from the catalog.)

Most flyfishers prefer chest-high waders, but you must be careful not to wade too deep.

WADING BOOTS

Some chest-high waders have wading boots attached (they're called boot-foot waders), but most just have a neoprene stocking foot. We recommend the stocking-foot type. A common problem with boot-foot waders is that the boots are often too wide, allowing your feet to slide around in them. You're much more likely to slip and fall in the water when that happens. The boots on boot-foot waders are also very heavy. Buying separate wading boots is a better way to go.

There are basically two styles of wading boots on the market. Some are lace-up and some have Velcro flaps to close them. We recommend the lace-up kind. The Velcro straps can come open more easily, causing you to lose a boot in the river. Above all, be sure that the boots have felt soles! Felt soles give you good traction on slippery rocks and are essential to your safety.

If you're shopping at a local store, you'll probably buy your boots at the same place you buy your waders. It's very important to wear the waders when you try on the boots. Don't guess about boot size and don't assume you can wear your regular shoe size. If you shop online or from a catalog, pay close attention to the company's sizing recommendations and be prepared to have to send the waders or the boots back if they don't fit. If your boots are too small, your feet will really hurt, and you'll be miserable while you're out fishing. If they're too large, your feet will slide around in them and you may fall.

If you outgrow your boots before you outgrow your waders, you can get a pair of bigger boots and often still wear your waders. If you outgrow your waders first, you can probably still use your boots with your new waders.

Girls who live in warm climates may not need to wear waders all the time, but they still need some sort of wading shoes or boots while they're "wet wading." Felt soles are still important for safety in rivers, even if the water is warm.

In lakes and along ocean beaches, felt soles aren't so important, but going barefoot or wearing regular sandals is not a good idea. Most ocean beaches are rocky, and many seashores have stinging creatures that live in the water or the sand. Glass or metal objects can also be dangerous to your feet. Some saltwater fly fishers wear a special bootie for wading that has a neoprene upper attached to a stiffer, stronger sole. Some wear the same type of water shoe that canoeists use, and some just wear an old pair of tennis shoes. If you're going to be wading in the surf, you'll need some kind of protection for your feet.

VESTS

Fly vests are handy for carrying fly boxes, clippers, split-shot, tippet spools, and all the other supplies you'll accumulate for fly fishing. Most people like a vest that also has a pocket in the back for a rain jacket, lunch sack, or water bottle.

Only a few vests are made small enough for young people. An extra-small size in some brands may be the best you can do. Just as with your waders and your wading boots, be sure to try on vests if you can. A vest that hangs below your waist will likely get wet, so a shorter one is probably better.

Girls in warm climates can enjoy "wet wadding," but they still need wading shoes or boots.

It's also important to put some fly boxes in the vest pockets, so you can see how it feels. That's the real test. Since most designers of fly vests aren't female, they don't always consider the fact that the placement of the pockets may put uncomfortable pressure on a woman's breasts. Further, when the pockets are full, a woman's breasts may force the vest far enough to the sides that it interferes with her casting.

Fly vests are optional. You don't have to use one, but you still need a way to carry your gear. Some fly fishers wear a waterproof fanny pack that can hold their water bottle and flies. You can slide the pack around to the front to get your fly box out. Others choose one of the new chest packs that hang around your neck and strap behind your back. Many women and girls don't like the chest packs, though, because they can be uncomfortable over your breasts.

Be sure to try on a vest to see how it feels.

To remedy all of this, some women just carry a small backpack for their equipment and flies. The only problem with that is, you'll have to take off the pack every time you want to get at your fly boxes. In fly fishing, like every thing else, there are always trade-offs. Knowing the options, however, will help you decide.

OUTERWEAR AND UNDERWEAR

It's bound to rain some of the time when you're out fishing, so you need to take along a rain jacket. You might be able to use the one that you already have, if it folds small enough to fit in a vest or pack. If you need to buy a rain jacket, you'll find that the ones made specifically for fly fishing are rather expensive. Some are cut extra short for deep wading, which you don't need right now. Others have as many pockets as a fly vest, which you also don't need.

Try catalogs like Cabela's for good-quality, inexpensive rainwear. Get a jacket that packs small and has as few seams as possible. Check to be sure the store or catalog has a money-back guarantee, so you can return the coat if it leaks. Whichever one you choose, make sure that it has a hood! Otherwise, water will be running down the back of your neck.

Beneath that rain jacket, you'll want to have a good, breathable fleece jacket or vest, windproof if possible. What about beneath that? Many girls and women forget just how important proper underwear is to their enjoyment of outdoor sports. When you're fly fishing, you're often standing in cold water all day long. It can be blowing, raining, or even sleeting, and you need to be prepared. A woman's core body temperature is lower than a man's, so we get colder quicker.

The secret to outdoor comfort for both women and men is layering. Starting from the skin out, the first layer of both top and bottom underwear should be a breathable fabric such as capilene or microfiber. That helps to wick moisture away from your body and keep you dry. The drier you are, the warmer you'll be. Over that, most people wear a shirt or turtleneck made of synthetic material. Whichever you choose, avoid clothes made exclusively of cotton if it's cold out. When cotton gets soaked, so do you.

If you'll be fishing in warmer climates, you won't need the layers, but everyone needs protection from the sun. Always wear a long-sleeved shirt and long pants to keep from getting sunburned. There are lots of great synthetic pants on the market today that have zip-off bottoms so they can be worn either as shorts or as pants.

TOP WEAR AND BOTTOM WEAR

Besides underwear, the other thing anglers tend to forget is their top wear. Always wear a hat to protect yourself from the sun and from the gear flying around in the air. For warm days, that usually means a baseball cap. (River Girls baseball caps are available at www.rivergirlsflyfishing.com.)

For cooler days you may well need more than just a cap. It's true that most of our body heat is lost from our heads. Wearing a hat is the best protection against loss of body temperature. Keep a wind-proof knit or fleece hat in the back of your vest for times when the wind comes up or a storm rolls in and the temperature drops.

A different kind of hat-one that covers your ears and the back of your neck is an absolutely essential piece of equipment for girls who will fish in sunny climates. A Large brimmed straw hat blows off too easily in the wind to be practical. Try one of the nylon baseball-style caps that have a drop-down shade to cover your ears and the back of your neck.

Last but not least, don't forget your feet. That's the other place we quickly lose heat from our bodies. Unless you're allergic to it, wool is the best and warmest type of sock to wear under your waders. Companies like Smartwool now make great wool socks without the itch. Once again, don't wear cotton if it's cold out. It provides absolutely no warmth, especially when wet.

If you don't find what you want at local stores, check out catalogs or visit online stores. A number of companies have shown an interest in developing gear

Always wear a long-sleeved shirt to keep from getting sunburned.

for young people, but no single company makes or provides all the gear you'll need at this time.

Waders, wading boots, and fly vests are the most difficult items to find in sizes for young people, and you'll have to shop around to find them all. You may find "youth" waders at one store but have to go to another store to find wading boots small enough. Some companies may have a "youth" fly vest, while others may have a women's fly vest in extra small that will fit just as well.

The following companies offer at least one model of waders, wading boots, or fly vests in "youth" sizes:

- Cabela's
- Dan Bailey
- Fitzwright Co./Bare Wading
- Fly Tech
- Hodgman
- Itasca
- L.L. Bean
- Orvis
- Pro Line
- Reddington
- Sportline
- Stearns

Most of these companies have web sites. Use Google or another search service to find their current web addresses. You should also do a search for fly fishing equipment for youth, because we predict that more and more companies will be making gear for young people in the future. More and more girls and boys are taking up fly fishing, so new products might have appeared by the time you read this book.

~

Okay, so there you have it. Gearing up for fly fishing isn't just about rods, reels, and fly lines. What you wear can go a long way toward ensuring that you have a great day out on the water.

A wading belt doesn't have to be fancy; it just needs to be snug to keep the water out.

CHAPTER 12

ON THE WATER: SAFETY AND COMFORT

I f you're going to be a fly fisher, then you're going to be wading in the water. You've already learned about what to wear as you wade, but there are other important things to consider when you're out there-namely your safety and well-being. Staying safe is no small matter. Neither is your overall comfort.

WADING

For safety in wading, let's start with a wading belt. In the last chapter, we looked at the features of chest-high waders. No matter which type of waders you choose, always be sure to cinch a wading belt tight around your waist. If you accidentally step into water too deep and aren't wearing a belt, your waders will fill with water and you won't be able to get back to shore safely. We hope this never happens to you, but like a seat belt in a car, your wading belt is there to protect you if it does happen. But you have to remember to wear it every time you wade.

Some models of waders include a belt, but you can use a belt you already have or an old one of your mom's or dad's. Some people use a backpack strap or a length of rope as a belt. It doesn't have to be fancy, just a snug fit to keep the water out.

In addition to wearing a belt, always keep in mind the limitations of waders. During her experiences fishing in rivers, Alex learned that chest-high waders are the preferred equipment for fly fishers. Even so, she sends along a safety warning.

Alex

Chest waders keep you totally dry, and you can go deeper in the water. But don't go too deep or the current might sweep you along.

Remember Alyssa's "scary dunkings" when she was small? Remember when Sam wanted chest-high waders? Her mom was worried that Sam might wade in too deep with chest-high waders. Wading too deep is easy to do when you get caught up in the fun and excitement of fly fishing. Sam made a promise that she'd never wade in deeper than her calves. That is our general recommendation for safe wading for you, too. Beyond that point, the river current may "sweep you along," as Alex says. In a lake, you're more apt to lose your balance when you're casting. Calf-high wading is a good rule to follow in any type of water.

Calf-high wading is a good rule to follow—don't wade deeper.

You may see other people more than knee-deep or even waist-deep in the water where you're fishing. Don't follow their example. They may be taller or heavier than you. Besides, guys can often wade to places where women can't. A guy's center of gravity is in his shoulders, while a woman's is in her hips. That makes the water push against our bodies in different ways. Your instincts will usually tell you when you're deep enough. Sometimes you'll be just ankle deep in fast water or near a sharp drop-off on the shore when you hear that little voice saying, "Don't go any deeper." Listen to it.

Wading Sticks

Wading sticks have been around for a long time. Maybe you've seen people searching the bank for a stick to use to help steady themselves as they cross a river. Well, these days it's smart to have your own wading stick that you always have with you when fishing rivers or creeks.

Several manufacturers now make wading sticks (or wading staffs, as they're sometimes called) that collapse like a tent pole and fit into a pouch that you wear on your wading belt. Any time you feel insecure in the water, you just pull your stick out of its pouch. It pops open and is ready to use. Most sticks have a cord that ties onto your wading belt, so the stick won't be lost in the current if you drop it.

Our favorite wading stick is one made by a woman-owned company. It's called a Folstaf. Most wading sticks come in a variety of models for people of different heights and weights.

Wading sticks give your two legs one additional anchor in the river. The increased stability they provide is great. Sam found that out one day as we were wading in some fairly shallow water. About halfway across the river, we came to a spot where the water was deeper. We both got out our sticks. I waded upstream of Sam to help break the current, and we continued across.

"Without my stick, I'm not sure I could have kept my feet on the bottom," Sam said. "I felt lots safer because I had it."

It's smart to have your own wading stick that you always have with you.

KEEPING YOUR HEAD ABOVE WATER

There are various flotation devices (life preservers) on the market. The most common style is called a life jacket or life vest. Always wear a life jacket when you're in a boat, whether you're on a lake, a river, or the ocean. No exceptions!

Wearing a flotation device of some sort is also an especially good idea when you're wading a deep river or one with swift currents. A simple fall, even in shallow water, can be life threatening when the current is strong. Bulky life jackets are difficult to manage when you're fly fishing, so most people opt for a life preserver that fits around your neck and inflates if you fall in.

Most wading sticks collapse and fit into a pouch on your wading belt.

These neck-flotation devices are commonly referred to as SOSpenders or "neck sausages." SOSpenders is the name of the company that is one of the largest producers of these devices.) They look like a pair of suspenders, and they fit behind your neck and fasten around your waist. Some models inflate by themselves, and others inflate by pulling a cord. Some models also have pockets for your supplies, so you don't have to wear a fishing vest.

You might end up having one type of life preserver for the boat and another for the river. Try several and wear the one that feels most comfortable. If it doesn't feel good, chances are that you won't wear it.

Always wear sunglasses when you're fishing.

SUNGLASSES AND A HAT

Two other safety devices that you need to wear are sunglasses and a hat.

Alex

Always wear sunglasses. That way you'll never get a fly in the eye. And be sure to look behind you constantly before casting so you don't hit anyone with your fly or your line.

As Alex says, you should always wear sunglasses when you're fly fishing. Not only do they protect your eyes, they also cut glare and help you see your footing under the water better, making wading safer.

Sunglasses with polarized lenses are by far the best at cutting glare off the water. Less glare will also mean fewer headaches, because you won't be squinting at the sun all day. Besides the safety issues, you'll also be able to see your fly and the fish better with polarized lenses, and that will help you catch more fish.

In addition to glasses, always wear a hat to protect your head from a fly that might snap back out of the tree or out of a fish. The bill or brim on a hat also protects against sun glare and sunburn.

No matter where you'll be fishing, you should protect both your eyes and your head. Alex's recommendation to always look behind you as you're casting is also good advice. You want to hook the fish, not another person.

SUNSCREEN AND BUG REPELLENT

Being outside most of the day can leave you pretty sunburned, even when it's cloudy. Your hat and a lightweight, long-sleeved shirt can help protect your skin, but always wear sunscreen when you're going to be out on the water all day. Many doctors recommend SPF 30 protection for all-day exposure. Put it on in the morning and then wash your hands thoroughly afterwards, because sunscreen is a "no-no" on your fly fishing equipment and flies. Carry some moist toilettes to wipe your hands if you re-apply the sunscreen later in the day. You don't want the oil or lotion on your fly line or your flies. There are often lots of bugs around when you're outdoors. Some are harmless, but some aren't. Many people have strong reactions to bug bites, so prevention is a good idea. A company named Cutters now makes an effective bug repellent in a rub-on stick, like your deodorant. That way you can rub it on your face and neck without getting any on your hands or your waders. The ingredient called "Deet" in bug repellent can ruin your fly line and your waders.

Believe it or not, the fish can smell both of these products. When they do, they'll avoid your fly like the plague.

Your hat and long-sleeved shirt can help protect your skin.

It's important to take a rest now and then.

WATER FOR YOU, NOT JUST THE FISH

Wearing waders and a vest can make you hot and sweaty when you're out on the water. But when you find that you're nauseous, weak, or dizzy as well, you could be the victim of heat exhaustion. That's why it's so important to take a rest now and then and to drink lots of water.

Always carry a water bottle when you're out fishing. Pop or soda doesn't count. It's plain water that will help keep you from getting dehydrated, and dehydration can contribute to heat exhaustion. It can also lead to hypothermia (loss of body temperature), as well as headaches, irritability, and other problems. Avoid it at all costs.

Women and girls often try to avoid drinking lots of fluids because of the difficulties that waders pose when a full bladder needs relief. Often a restroom is not available nearby. So, where does a girl go when she has to "go?"

All fly fishers get used to using outhouses or the bushes. Just carry some toilet paper and a zip-lock bag for disposal, so you never, never, never leave toilet paper in the woods. It won't seem like such a big problem, if you're prepared. Never hesitate to ask if there is a toilet or "head" on a boat. If not, insist on having a bucket available that you can use. People who fish and do other outdoor activities are used to asking others to turn around while they "go." Obviously, it's easier for guys than for us, but once you do it, you'll find it's less stressful than you think.

Many girls and women are reluctant to go fishing when they have their menstrual period. Don't stay home and miss all the fun. Rather, prepare ahead of time and tell your mom or dad that you'll be menstruating so they can help you figure out how to handle it. Generally, menstruating women try to wear tampons rather than pads, if they can, when they're going fishing. A couple of extra ones can easily fit into a pocket in your vest. Once again, some plastic sandwich bags can be used to take them home for disposal.

River girls don't let these inconveniences get in their way. Overall, the good times outweigh the difficulties. Most agree that a day on the water makes it worth putting up with such things.

WHISTLES AND OTHER SAFETY DEVICES

Most fly fishers carry a whistle in their vests for times when they want to signal that they're in trouble or to help locate their fishing partner. The noise of rushing water makes it almost impossible for other people to hear you call out to them, but they can usually hear a whistle. Some families or groups use short-range walkie-talkies or two way radios.

People who are going to be fishing in a wilderness location also carry a small tarp called a "space blanket." They use it to warm up someone who has gotten chilled. Space blankets have been credited with saving people's lives. It's also a good idea to have a warm hat and gloves in the back pocket of your vest, in case the weather turns cold. Remember the rule that you lose most of your body heat through your head. Hypothermia can strike very quickly, so be prepared.

Depending on where you're going fishing, there will most likely be a first-aid kit in the car or on the boat or in someone's backpack. It really doesn't take much to carry the basics, such as band-aids, bandages, or antihistamine tablets for a bee sting. If someone needs them, you'll be glad you have them along.

FISHING BY YOURSELF

Sam remembers always having to wait for someone to take her fishing when she was little because her mom wouldn't let her go by herself. She used to think it was just because her mom was really strict. Now that she's older, she realizes that the risk of falling into the water with no one to rescue her or the possibility of meeting a wild animal on the trail are what made her mom so cautious.

PART THREE ~ OTHER ESSENTIALS

Sam is allowed to fish the river by herself now that she is a teenager, but her mom still requires that she stay within a certain, well-defined area and that there are other people around.

Sam

I didn't used to think much about safety when I was fishing, but now I understand better that the water can be risky, that there are certain precautions that are wise to take, and That I have to pay attention. I'm more conscious of what to do because I want to be around to fish in the future.

Sam has the right idea about safety. Taking basic safety precautions is essential to having an enjoyable day of fly fishing and staying around for more. You wouldn't go rollerblading without knee pads and a helmet, and you wouldn't go kayaking minus a life vest. So, don't go fly fishing without considering your personal safety.

Sunburn or dehydration can spoil your day fast. A wading accident can be even more serious. Taking these few extra safety steps creates the right conditions for having fun, not problems.

The risk of falling into the water with on one to rescue you makes parents cautious.

PART FOUR

Our Past and
Our Future

Many other women have followed in her footsteps.

CHAPTER 13

FROM THE BEGINNING

From the very beginning, women were interested in fly fishing. Most people don't know that a woman is believed to have written the very first book on flies and fly fishing way back in the fifteenth century! Even more surprising, she was a nun.

Her name was Dame Juliana Berners, and her book was titled Treatyse of Fysshynge wyth an Angle (that's the way they spelled things in the 1400s). The book gave anglers guidance on everything from how to build a fly rod to designing the best flies for different times of the year. Pretty remarkable, huh?

Fly fishing women consider Dame Juliana to be the mother of fly fishing. Many other women have followed in her footsteps.

In 1876 Sara Jane McBride, a self-educated entomologist (someone who studies bugs) and prize-winning Dy-tier, wrote the first American papers on the life cycles of insects from an angler's point of view. Just a few years later, Mary Orvis Marbury, the daughter of the founder of the famous Orvis Company, compiled and authored the first complete book on American fishing flies, called Favorite Flies and Their Histories. It became an instant bestseller when it appeared in 1892.

Cornelia "Fly Rod" Crosby, famed for her hunting and fishing skills, was one of this country's first outdoor writers. Her articles gained national attention in the late 1800s, as she traveled the Northeast on the Maine Central Railroad with her custom-made fly rod and birch-bark canoe.

More recently, Joan Wulff, often referred to as one of the "living legends" of fly fishing today, has written several books on fly-casting techniques and continues to operate her own fly fishing schools.

The wonderful accomplishments of these and other women who made fishing history can be found in the book, Reel Women, by Lyla Foggia. Many of the book's stories are about fly fishers, and their pictures and stories will delight and entertain you. It's a great way to learn about your heritage as a fly fisher.

River women share their love of fly fishing
by teaching and modeling patience.

CHAPTER 14

BECOMING A RIVER WOMAN

Fly fishing is at the heart of a river woman. In fly fishing she finds peace and fantastic experiences in our natural world. It's an important part of her existence, something that helps ease life's stresses and brings a sense of the interrelationships between all living creatures.

River women share their love of fly fishing with others, both young and old. New fly fishers are developed and nurtured through their efforts. They teach and model patience and other characteristics required of a successful fly fisher. Through them we see how fun fly fishing is and why it's so satisfying. They help others understand the need for conserving and protecting our fish and the habitat in which they live.

Not every river woman started out as a river girl, but we want to introduce you to a few who did. They tell wonderful stories about their beginnings and what fly fishing has meant to them over the years. Here's how some of them became river women.

ELLIE

Ellie is a retired university professor. Her dad taught her to fly fish when she was only three years old. She yanked so hard on the first fish she caught that it flew out of the water and hit her dad in the face! He didn't really mind. He loved that his daughter was learning to fly fish and took Ellie and her sister fishing all the time.

By elementary school she had her own three-piece bamboo fly rod and had learned to tie flies to replace the ones she lost in trees. (That's still a problem for all of us.) She was lucky enough to spend summers in a cabin on a lake in the California Sierras, where she got lots of time with her dad and lots of time to practice.

Reflecting back, she reports that many of her fly fishing skills came from spending countless hours with her dad and his fishing buddies.

"I learned a lot more than just casting," she says. "I found out that, no matter how wet, cold, and hungry you are, you keep on fishing and don't complain. Or that you may get skunked today, but if you hang in there, your turn will come to land the big one."

Many of the lessons from these fishing trips served her well, she reports, when she later worked in an all-male department at a college.

"I was able to hold my own with the guys to gain their respect." With that ability, she worked for many years only with men in the college's athletic department and built a women's athletic program while she was there.

"As a child, I felt my fishing skill was a positive thing," she recalls. "People would say, 'Look at the fish the little girl caught.'" As a teenager, she thought maybe it was a liability, because "nice girls wear skirts and go to parties; they don't handle slimy fish." As she grew older, however, she realized that was not the case.

Fly fishing was a great way to be outdoors, like the guys were. She now describes her fishing skills as an asset, and her fly fishing passion as an obsession.

"My greatest fishing thrill is luring a large fish up from the bottom of the pool to smash my fly on the surface."

"Fly fishing takes me to beautiful settings," Ellie responds when asked what fly fishing has meant to her over her life. "That's one of the special, lifelong pleasures of fly fishing. While I'm out there, I can find a special connection with wonderful, natural places."

These days Ellie frequently finds herself in the role of mentor to other women getting started as fly fishers.

"There's always something new to learn," she says, "both for them and for me. That's the beauty of fly fishing." Spoken like a true river woman.

Fly fishing takes us to beautiful settings.

BETH-ANNE

Girls typically learn to fly fish from their dads, as Ellie did, but not always. One woman told us that her older brother taught her. Beth-Anne was privileged to learn from her grandmother.

"My first fly fishing experience was in the early 1960s when my grandmother, Margaret Glidewell, taught me and all of her grandchildren to fish," she says. "My fondest memories are of my youth, when l was five or six, staying at the cabin and fishing next to my Mom mom, as we called her."

Beth-Anne remembers that her grandmother would hold her hand until a fish bit so she could learn how to set the hook so "he" didn't get away. After "he" was hooked, her grandmother would make her try to land "him."

"Fish were always referred to with male pronouns by Mommom," Beth-Anne recalls. One of Beth-Anne's clearest memories is of getting saved from drowning by her Mommom.

"l had a great big catfish on the end of my line," she remembers. "Grandmother grabbed me just as that fish was pulling my little body into the water, because I refused to let go of the rod."

In spite of everything, they landed the fish, and her grandmother proclaimed it the largest catfish ever caught in those waters!

"She taught me a lot about fishing and even more about just enjoying nature and the world we live in," Beth-Ann says. Mommom also was a skilled fly-tier.

"She would make homemade flies back then from the darnedest things," Beth-Ann recalls. "When l was small I thought they looked weird, but now I wish she were alive to teach me her own patterns. l have learned to tie flies now, in my forties, but none of the 'refined' flies I tie compare to the ones she would invent herself. I was too young then to remember how she tied them, but I wish I had paid more attention."

One day, Mommom took Beth-Anne and her brother fishing on one of the best trout streams in the area. The only problem was that the land on both sides was owned by an elderly lady who would bring her shotgun out and threaten people until they moved on down the stream.

"We waded in with Mommom and were catching quite a few trout when out came Martha, who told us to move along or she'd shoot. I still can see the look on my grand mother's face as she grinned and told her, 'We were just leaving, Martha. We've caught enough for supper anyway. Now put your gun away 'cause my grandkids are with me, and if you ever wave that gun around any kids again, I'll give you a reason to shoot at me!'"

Beth-Anne's mother still owns the 177 acres and cabin that belonged to her parents (Mommom and Poppop), with streams that still hold wild brook and

Some girls are privileged to learn fly fishing from a river woman.

brown trout. Her family has most of the antique bamboo rods her grandmother used and taught her on. She even has some of her grandparents' old fishing catalogs-one dating back to the 1930s-and an original edition of Mary Orvis Marbury's famous book about flies.

It's obvious what Beth-Anne's family history of fly fishing has meant to her. More than just a connection to her ancestors, it's a legacy that, as a river woman, she plans to carry down to future generations.

"I may never be the fisherwoman my grandmother was," she says, "but I keep practicing, with high hopes that in six or seven years I can teach my soon-to-be-born first grandchild the same love of fishing and the outdoors that my Mommom taught me."

SELINE

"I was introduced to fly fishing by my Norwegian father and my grandfather. In Norway, my great uncles, grandfather, father, and I would fish at the family cabins and on the Laerdal River. As a kid, I would sit on the rocks and catch trout and watch the people land Atlantic salmon."

So, started Seline's lifelong passion for fly fishing. She proudly received her first fly wallet around the age of nine. Now she had a place to keep her flies, just like the grown-ups had. About that same time, she learned that a rod was only to be cast outside the house, when she hooked her grandmother's dress while they were in the kitchen.

In fly fishing we find peace and fantasic expeirences in our natural world.

Over the years, Seline became a saltwater fisher for bluefish and bass on Long Island and a spear fisher on St. Croix, in the U.S. Virgin Islands. Fly fishing returned as a major part of her life again about ten years ago. Her mother was beginning to fly fish then in California, and they loved heading off to the river together. Sadly, Seline's mom was battling breast cancer.

"Although she lost her battle in 1996," Seline says, "fly fishing brought her great peace during her struggle." Through that experience Seline gained a whole new under standing of the value of this satisfying sport for women of all ages and in all circumstances.

Now, Seline's whole life revolves around fly fishing. She is the executive director of a fly fishing program for breast cancer survivors called Casting for Recovery. CFR, as it's called, offers weekend retreats all over the country where breast cancer survivors, young and old alike, can learn to fly fish and make it part of their recovery. They are discovering the satisfaction that can be gained from learning a new skill. They also find that cancer does not necessarily mean the end of life or of wonderful opportunities to be outdoors. Now that's a great way to be a river woman!

ANN

Ann's story is so beautiful that I'll repeat it here pretty much as she told it to me. I think you'll see how marvelous it was for her to learn to fly fish and also what it has meant to her throughout her life. As you'll see, she's passing on the skills she's learned, as well as the appreciation she developed for the "wholeness" of fly fishing.

When I Was A Fly fishing Girl

As a young girl of nine, there were two adult activities that I yearned to be considered "grown-up enough" to participate in. One was billiards. The other was fly fishing. Both were the domain of my grandfather, whom I loved and admired enormously. And these were the two activities he was passionate about, these and riding horseback.

We had a pretty little creek on our ranch. No more than nine feet wide (usually more like five or six), it meandered through the hayfields. There were stretches

The creek ran cold and clear into deep, dark pools of calm water.

where the Rocky Mountain snowmelt, cold and clear as could be, ran shallow over a pebbled creek bottom and then turned into deep, dark pools of calm water with overhanging banks. There were willows everywhere. The grass was mostly timothy. It was lush and smelled so fresh, warmed by the morning sun.

When my family picnicked there, I'd sit by the banks and daydream, lost in the smells of the earth and the water, in the sounds of the creek, in the complete peacefulness of green grasses, tall spruce, and clear blue sky.

One morning, I got up to watch Grandad as he readied his rod and creel. He was going to fish the beaver dams that day. I begged to go along. He had taught my mother to fish when she was little, why not his granddaughter now? I was in luck! He said yes, I could come and learn. First, however, he had me watch as he put his rod together, then mounted the reel properly, threaded the line and leader, and tied on a tiny dry fly with what I knew was the tiniest knot I had ever seen.

Grandad explained that knowing, preparing, and maintaining one's equipment was as important as casting and catching. He had great love for–and took great care with his equipment. There was a real reverence I sensed for the vintage split-bamboo rod. In his old aluminum fly box, all the fly barbs were inserted "just so," side-by-side into the cork strips. Every little detail had his full attention. I was mesmerized!

He made things easy for me and demonstrated how I was to put on a larger wet fly. I found it easy to attach to the leader because all I had to do was pass the fly's nylon leader-end loop through the line's leader-end loop, thread the fly back through its own loop, and pull tight. I could do that! I felt very proud.

When we came near the dams, we crouched down and snuck through the tall grass, being silent so the trout wouldn't hear us. This was difficult as I had so many questions. I did it, though, because I sensed my fishing trip with him would end abruptly if I spoke out. I also learned one had to pay attention not to make shadows on the water, which would alert any trout to danger and distract them from taking our flies. There was more to fly fishing than I had imagined.

Once home, he drew a circle out on the dirt road and had me stand back and cast the fly into it. Later, we cast together, one at a time, at a rock he placed under a bush. Of course, the bush represented the multitude of willows on the stream banks that had snagged my flies so often that morning. I had to get my hook out of that bush time after time. He made it all fun by making it a contest.

The next day my mother took me fishing with her. I had never seen her have such a wonderful time. She just loved the stream! I'll never forget how she would roll up her jeans almost to her knees and wade in with her old Keds to painstakingly untangle a fly caught in willow branches on the other side. Often it seemed to her better to frighten the fish from the hole we were fishing than to snap the line and lose the fly.

I watched and learned and must have done okay, because then she took me again and again that summer. I believe it was the best thing we ever did together. Midday, when the fish were not feeding, she and Dad might take all of us, my brothers and me, for a picnic to a section of stream that was shallow but showed promise, and we'd wade in and build rock dams. The backed-up water gave the trout deeper holes. We called ourselves the creek engineers and had a great time of it. Of course, we'd return another day to fish these new holes, just to see if our "engineering" had attracted bigger fish. And we were often pleased with the results of our efforts!

Those days, in the 1950s, a license allowed you to keep fish measuring eight inches, and since a creek no bigger than ours rarely supported a fish larger than twelve inches, we put many ten inchers in our creels to take home for breakfast. Of course, we learned to clean them ourselves and each time were eager to see if we had caught a female with roe (eggs) or a male, which we were happier about,

When a river woman wants inspiration, she takes
a friend or a child, and they go find a little stream.

as roe would become little finger lings. Being responsible for new life in the creek was a privilege, we were taught.

You never forget the childhood moments that bring great joy or great fear. Anything to do with fly fishing, even just being near a stream, triggers in me the feeling of pride in accomplishment of an art and a belonging to and a responsibility for looking after something natural and as incredibly beautiful as that flowing water and the life swimming in it.

So now, when I want inspiration or to let my mind unwind, I take a friend or a child, and we go and find a little stream.

CHAPTER 15

YOU ARE THE FUTURE

The future of fly fishing depends on you and me, as well as the river girls Samantha, Blair, Alyssa, and Alex-and older fly fishers such as Ellie, Beth-Ann, Seline, and Ann. It's up to all of us to help preserve our environment and our waters as places where wild fish can live and flourish. That's true whether we're thinking of lakes, rivers, or even the ocean.

It's pretty simple: the more our waters are polluted, the less fish we're going to be able to fish for. That means that we have to get out there and help with restoration of fish habitat and work on efforts to dean up our streams. We can't leave it up to someone else.

For fly fishing to have a future we also need to practice conservation with our present fish supply so that we don't overfish them. Some salmon have become extinct in the Pacific Northwest because of overfishing, and wild Arctic grayling, once abundant in the upper Midwest, are now gone, due to environmental damage and probably overfishing.

Practicing conservation doesn't mean you can't ever eat a fish you catch, like Alyssa and Samantha and most fly fishers have done. Rather, it means learning and following the fishing rules and regulations that are in place to help preserve the health and diversity of wild fish.

"Limit your kill, don't kill your limit" is a good slogan to follow.

Practicing conservation also means releasing your fish correctly. The famous fly fisher Lee Wulff once said, "A fish is too valuable to be caught only once." Since then people have come to realize that there is not an infinite supply of fish. Our fish are a limited resource. Releasing a fish correctly can help ensure that it is there for you or someone else to enjoy another time.

Alex

I hate keeping fish. My dad hates it, his dad hated it, and I've grown up the same way. I only keep fish if I absolutely have to.

Fortunately for us and for the fish, practicing catch-and-release is easier for fly fishers. The fish is caught on a single, barbless hook, rather than the more damaging treble hooks used by spin fishers. And unlike bait fishing, the hook is usually in the fish's lip or just inside the mouth, rather than swallowed, making removal easier and quicker.

After a long fight, you often have to revive a fish by holding it in the water until it's ready to swim away. Have someone help you the first few times you revive a fish to make sure you're doing it correctly. It is your responsibility to spend whatever time it takes to rejuvenate your fish. It will be worth it when you feel that fish dart from your hand heading back to its watery world after the fun you had together.

Blair

I really don't like to keep the fish. Releasing it makes me feel better about myself. I enjoy just the fishing, not keeping the fish.

Several national fly fishing organizations, state departments of fish and wildlife, and other fishing organizations have worked together to develop a uniform set of guidelines for the practice of catch-and-release.

You're a river girl now and a fly fisher. Alex, Alyssa, Blair, and Samantha, our river girls, can't wait for you to join them.

"You'll love fly fishing," Alyssa promises. "It's very relaxing and challenging. Besides, you'll get a real charge when you catch your first fish."

"Fly fishing is really fun to learn, and it's an exciting sport," Alex adds. "Give it a try! You won't be sorry."

As a river girl and, later, as a river woman, you'll be among those who help preserve our fisheries, our environment, and our sport. Flyfishers will look to your generation to write the next books about fish, about new flies and new techniques for using them, and about the incredible places where we earthlings interact with those silvery waterlings.

Whatever Happened to Samantha, Blair, Alex and Alyssa
The Original River Girls

What Ever Happened to: Samantha

Samantha Dubin, the girl whose picture graces the cover of the original River Girls book, says that at thirty years old she is now doing what she always dreamed of doing, being in the medical world. She is a doctor. After the grueling studies of earning a bachelor's degree, she then attended dental school in California,

PRACTICING CATCH-AND-RELEASE

Landing Your Catch
- Use as strong a line as practical to bring in the fish as quickly and carefully as possible.
- Avoid removing the fish from the water. Do not let it flop around in shallow water, on rocks, or on dry land.
- Use nets made with soft. knotless mesh for bigger fish.

Removing the Hook
- Use single hooks and flatten down the barbs with pliers to make removal easier.
- Remove the hook quickly and gently, while keeping the fish in the water.
- Use needle-nosed pliers or a hemostat, if necessary, and back the hook out the way it went in.
- If a fish is hooked deeply, don't try to unhook the fly. Cut your leader and leave the fly in the fish rather than injure the fish. The hook will rust out.
- Avoid using stainless-steel hooks. They don't rust out as easily as other hooks do if left in a fish.

Handling Your Catch
- Wet your hands before handling fish to protect the slimy coating.
- Never squeeze a fish.
- Cradle the fish in the water with one hand under its belly while your other hand grips its body tightly right in front of the tail.
- Keep your fingers away from the fish's gills.
- Support the fish in the water, removing it only briefly while someone takes a picture.

Reviving Your Catch
- Support the fish upright in the water with one hand under the belly and one hand encircling the body right in front of the tail.
- Point the fish's mouth into the current and hold the fish there until its gills are working well and it can maintain its balance.
- Do not let go of the fish until it actually thrusts itself out of your hand. (A fish released too soon may roll belly-up and drown. Remember this rule: the fish decides when it's ready to be released, not you.)

receiving her D.M.D., after which she went on to medical school, and received her M.D. She is currently in her fourth of six years of post-graduate residency training in oral and maxillofacial surgery in Detroit, MI.

Sam is also married to a great guy named Nick, who completed medical school as well and is currently in residency training for orthopedic surgery. They had a wonderful wedding in Alaska in 2015 and family and friends were delighted to get to meet the groom. Although they were lucky enough to obtain residencies in the same hospital, that doesn't mean that they have the same schedule, Sam says. But they're making it work.

Sam is having trouble living in southeast Michigan, which she calls the "most difficult place I've ever lived. It's gray all the time and there aren't even any rivers or mountains to look at." They do have friends with whom they manage to head to the rivers and hiking trails in northern Michigan from time to time, but Sam says, "I'm glad that I have to be inside for my work all the time or I might go nuts!"

Sam was always an "outside girl." She loves fishing hiking, skiing and other outdoor sports, but her favorite is, and always will be fly fishing. She put her heart and soul into the creation of the original River Girls book. Because she was an Alaska girl living and working at her mother's fishing lodge, I had lots of opportunities to film her as we wrote the original book.

"Reading about Maxine now reminds me so much of myself at that age," Samantha says. ("She is much more talented than I ever was, of course, she adds). It's difficult to explain the feeling that you get when it's only you on a river with a fly rod but it's so special, unique, and undiscovered by so many. Most importantly, it is something that was not accessible for young girls and women until relatively recently.

"At 30 years old, to be able to watch a talented young woman like Maxine out-stage men and women alike makes me proud as both a woman and as a fly fisher. She is continuing to pave the way for women in a male-dominated field, something I am all too familiar with as a surgeon. She is a bright light and reminder to all of us that there is nothing we can't do. And I also just want to give a final shout out to Pudge, for being not only an exceptional fly fisher but an amazing role model who helped shape me into the strong woman I am today."

While Sam's career goal was always doing something in "doctoring," she says that she always intends to "circle back to fly fishing." She has plans to make a short visit to Alaska later in the summer to see her mom and brother and do some fly fishing. The fly rods are already rigged and waiting. "I'm going to make a fly fisher out of Nick, too (who wasn't able to join her, unfortunately) just as soon as I can. A fly rod is in our closet just waiting for that," she promises. Nick says he'll be ready and waiting when that time comes.

Whatever Happened to: Blair

Blair, Alex's cousin, went on from mastering and practicing the art of fly fishing to become enamored of other sports like lacrosse and soccer throughout high school and college. Ultimately, she became the captain of her school's women's lacrosse team and then her college team at the University of Virginia as well.

The U of V is where Blair met her husband, Greg, who just happened to compete on the men's soccer team (winning a national championship in '09), and it was love at first sight. Now they are both teaching at the Norfolk Academy in Virginia Beach, VA, and have been for six years. Greg is the school's coach and Blair teaches middle school English as well as coaching the varsity lacrosse team.

Eighteen months ago, their daughter, "Mo-Mo" came into their lives. She quickly got the nick-name from Mount Morgan, a mountain near their families' summer home on Squam Lake in central New Hampshire. Blair hopes to have other children as time goes on, but right now they are having a blast with their first, Morgan.

Blair and her cousin Alex both have large families, and one of their most treasured times is summer, when the family congregates in the large family cabin on the lake and enjoys the hiking, canoeing, fly fishing and all of the other sports that a beautiful state like theirs offers.

Blair told me that she often takes her fly rod out in the lake to fish, baby and all, and recently Greg said that he would like to try it out. He did, and after getting the hang of it, told her that they will have to do more of it. I didn't hear if he landed a fish or not. It sounded like Mo-Mo enjoyed it too.

Maxine McCormick is quite a surprise to Blair, but being the athletic person that she is, she couldn't wait to hear more about Maxine, and follow her accomplishments in the world of fly fishing. I directed Blair to all of the internet and YouTube footage available, and she, like most other people, can hardly believe that Maxine has won all the national and international championships before even graduating from high school. Blair certainly intends to follow Maxine's fly fishing career while picking up her own fly rod whenever she can and, hopefully getting Greg to come along with her.

Whatever Happened to: Alex

Of the four original River Girls, the one who has taken her interest in fly fishing and made a career out of it is Alex. At thirty years old she has already developed various activities for herself in the fly-fishing industry. She works as an independent consultant for outdoor-focused companies and nonprofits. Her clients include *Tail Fly Fishing Magazine,* a magazine focused on fly fishing in salt water, for which she is a consulting editor and does digital marketing. Other of her clients include Fay Ranches, a larger ranch brokerage that sells sporting properties, and Megafin Expeditions, a fishing travel company specializing in extreme expeditions.

Alex also participates Now or Neverglades, a coalition of non-profit organizations working to address problems in Florida's Everglades, and restoration and advocacy work.

Alex has also conducted seminars and presentations, written for several different outdoor publications including *Tail,* and hosted fly-fishing trips all over the world. She lists Bolivia, Alaska, the Bahamas, Cuba, Belize, Argentina, Mexico, and Montana as some of her favorite destinations, though one of her preferred places to fish remains her backyard in the Florida Keys and Biscayne Bay. She spends much of her free time there as well as traveling to fish, often with her dad.

Alex has come a long way since learning to fly fish at the age of eight, just as Maxine did, and she plans to continue fly fishing as often as she can for the rest of her life. She's delighted to learn about Maxine and her success in the fly casting universe saying "It's great to see a young woman like Maxine excelling in fly casting. She's beating women and men with decades more experience through her talent and her dedication to the sport. I'm sure there are big things in her future, and she's certainly showing other girls that they can do whatever they put their minds to."

Whatever Happened to: Alyssa

Alyssa was the oldest of the original River Girls. She is now married and an OB/GYN physician, completing her residency at the Mayo Clinic, a nonprofit academic medical center based in Rochester, Minnesota. Congratulations, Alyssa! We wish you the best and hope that fly fishing is still a sport that will stay in your life forever.

I'm astounded to realize that two out of the original four River Girls have now become doctors. All four of them are certainly contributing to their world in their own way, and Maxine is following in hers.

A SHOPPING GUIDE FOR GEARING UP

A s with many sports, buying fly fishing equipment can be costly. You may need to collect the pieces over a period of time. The good news is that your equipment will last you for years and years, some it for your entire life, if you take good care of it. Here are a couple of tips for buying smart.

Start out by reviewing Chapter 4: Gearing Up: Fly Rod, Fly Reel, and Fly Line. After doing your homework and deciding what equipment you want, shop around and check the prices of items in stores and catalogs so you can see what you like and what you can afford. Just remember, however, that price isn't everything. It's more important to get the rod that is right for you, for instance, even if it means saving just a little bit longer to be able to afford it. The checklist below will help you in your search.

Once you know prices, then you can plan for getting what you need right away and what you can wait for. You might buy one item with your own money and ask your folks for another item for your birthday or Christmas. Maybe your parents and your grandparents would be willing to go together to buy more expensive items on your list. Lots of stores have waders, boots, and vests available in the spring at pretty reason able prices. It can be a good time to shop.

Sam got her gear a little bit at a time. When she started fly fishing, she certainly didn't have all the different weights of rods she uses now. So, decide what you're going to fish for most, get the rod, reel, and line for that type of fishing, and you're almost ready to go!

FISHING LICENSE

You'll also need to check with the store to see if you need a fishing license. Most states have an age limit. Be sure to follow whatever requirements your state puts on your license, such as displaying it on the outside of your clothes or having it on your person at all times when you're fishing. You should also be given a copy of the state fishing regulations when you buy your license. Read the ones that apply to the place where you'll be fishing so you'll know what the rules are for that spot.

ACCESSORIES

In addition to your basic equipment-rod, reel, line, leader, vest or pack, and waders-it's a good idea to stock your vest with the things that you're going to need while you're out fishing. Some of the most important things are on the shopping list, such as an extra spool of tippet material and clippers to cut off a fly or a piece of tippet. Needle-nosed pliers or hemostats (pinchers like doctors use) will help you hold a small fly or remove a hook from a fish's mouth.

The stuff called "floatant" is a sort of gel-like substance that you rub on your dry fly to help it float. Most dry-fly anglers consider it essential. It comes in a tiny tube that you can usually hook right on your vest so that it is handy when you need it. Split-shot are tiny balls of lead that can be attached to your leader to make your nymph or streamer sink faster and drift lower in the water.

You'll see that we've put polarized sunglasses and bug repellent on the list as well. You should always wear glasses or sunglasses when you're fishing. When it comes to "bug juice," try to get the stuff that comes in a rub-on stick, so you don't get it on your hands. The best stick is made by Cutters. If you must buy a lotion or spray, just be very sure to never, never get it on your fishing equipment or your fly. The Deet in it will actually ruin the materials. Be especially careful with the spray. We've also added sunscreen, another product that you should avoid getting on your equipment or flies.

FLIES

Of course, if you know some of the flies that you'll need for the fishing you'll be doing, then you should buy three or four of each of them and an inexpensive, basic fly box to put them in as well. (You can order an inexpensive fly box at www. rivergirlsfly fishing.com.)

If you're going fishing with your mom or dad or someone else, be sure to ask if they will have the flies for you to use. Don't just assume they will. If they say no, then ask for recommendations on a couple of the best flies to get for your outing.

There are several other items on the checklist, and you may need to look back at previous chapters to refresh your memory about them. You may want to add other things you see in shops or catalogs that you think will help you catch more fish.

Now you're ready to go shopping!

A FLYFISHING EQUIPMENT SHOPPING GUIDE AND CHECKLIST
(Take this with you when you go shopping)

EQUIPMENT	COMMENTS	✔
• ROD: BRAND AND MODEL		
Cost		
Length: 8', 8 1 /2 ', or 9'		
Action: medium or medium-fast		
Line weight: 4, 5, or 6 for average fish		
Line weight: 7, 8, or 9 for larger fish		
Metal or pvc rod tube		
Cloth sleeve		
Guarantee/return policy		
• REEL: BRAND AND MODEL		
Cost		
Adequate drag/adjustment		
Palming rim		
Right or left wind available		
Anodized for use in salt water		
Extra spools available		
Easy spool release		
• LINE: BRAND AND MODEL		
Cost		
Type: weight-forward floating		
Weight: to match rod		
Type: sink-tip (if needed)		
Sink rate: intermediate		
Sink length: 12'-14'		
Weight: to match rod		
• LEADERS: BRAND		
Length: 6-½' or 7-'/,'		
X-number/pound test		
Tippet spool: to match leader		

EQUIPMENT	COMMENTS	✔
• FLIES		
Dry flies/size		
Nymphs/size		
Streamers/size		
Poppers/size		
Saltwater flies/size		
• ACCESSORIES		
Fly box		
Clippers		
Hemostat or needle-nosed pliers		
Fly floatant		
Split-shot		
Hook sharpener		
Polarized sunglasses		
Insect repellent		
Sunscreen		
• WADERS: BRAND AND TYPE		
Cost		
Size		
• FELT-SOLED WADING BOOTS: BRAND		
Cost		
Size		
Lace-up closure		
• FISHING VEST OR PACK: BRAND		
Cost		
Size		
• SAFETY/COMFORT ITEMS		
Wading stick		
Life jacket/SOSpenders		
Rain jacket with hood		
Hat		
Water bottle		
First-aid items		

• FISHING LICENSE (IF REQUIRED)

APPENDIX 2
GLOSSARY OF FLYFISHING TERMS

Most of the terms defined here are used in the book, but we've added some common fly fishing words and phrases that you might hear or read and not understand as a beginner.

Action, fly-rod: The degree of flex in a fly rod. Fast-action rods flex only near the tip, medium-action rods about a third of the way down, and slow-action rods about halfway down.

Anadromous: Describing fish that hatch in fresh water, migrate to the ocean, live most of their lives there, and return to fresh water to spawn. Salmon, steelhead, and char are examples of anadromous species.

Backcast: The movement of the fly line in the air behind the fly fisher during casting.

Backing: Braided line attached between the fly line and the reel. Used to help fill up the spool and to allow fish to make runs longer than the length of the fly line.

Barb: The upward-slanted projection of metal near the point of the hook. Flattening the barb with needle-nosed pliers forms a barbless hook.

Bead-head: A fly, usually a nymph, with a metal or glass bead slid onto the hook to a point just behind the hook eye.

Bucktail: Hair from a deer's tail used in the wings and tails of many artificial flies.

Butt. fly-rod: The bottom, thick section of the fly rod covered by the cork handle and reel seat.

Butt, leader: The heavy end of a tapered leader, the end connected to the fly line.

Caddisfly: A common, moth-like aquatic insect that is one of the most important food sources for fish. Adults fold their wings over their backs in a tent shape.

Cast: The act of moving the fly rod in a way that sends the fly line and fly out onto the water.

Cast. false: In an overhead cast, the preliminary movement of the fly line and fly backward and forward without the fly hitting the water or the ground; used to lengthen the line to be cast, change direction, or dry the fly prior to casting.

Cast, overhead: A type of cast that moves the line backward and forward in the air in preparation for delivering the fly to the water.

Cast, roll: A type of cast that moves the line forward without a backcast; used to keep the fly away from obstructions behind the caster.

Channel: A slot formed by the current that directs water along a certain path.

Char: A group of fish related to trout, e.g. Dolly Varden, Arctic char, and brook trout.

Chum: A species of Pacific salmon. Males develop red stripes along their sides when spawning. Also referred to as "dog" salmon.

Current: Water flow caused by gravity or, in areas near salt water, by tides.

Dead drift: A fly fishing technique that enables the fly to float downstream naturally with the current, unimpeded by line or leader, in imitation of natural insects.

Downstream: The direction in which river water flows away from the angler.

Drag: When water currents, wind, or the leader cause the fly to drift in a manner different from the way a real insect or bait fish would behave. Also, the braking device on a fishing reel.

Drag-free: The condition of drifting naturally on the surface of the water.

Drift: Movement of a dry fly on the surface of the water. Also, to be transported or moved from one location to another by action of the water, as with a drift boat.

Dry fly: A type of artificial fly designed to imitate a winged insect floating on the water.

Emerger: The stage of an aquatic insect when it moves to the surface of the water and prepares to hatch into a winged adult.

Feeding lane: A narrow line of the current that carries food to a fish.

Feeding lie: The location in a river where a fish waits for food to drift by. (See hold.)

Floatant: A substance that waterproofs dry flies to prolong their buoyancy.

Fly rod: A particular type of fishing rod designed to cast a fly line. Usually made of graphite, it is typically longer and more tapered than other types of fishing rods.

Float tube: A floating device in which the angler sits and paddles around a lake or pond; also known as a "belly boat."

Fly line: A type of fishing line designed to be cast by a fly rod. It is comprised of a core and a coating that can be modified to meet specific fishing needs.

Fly line, floating: A fly line that is constructed so it remains on the water's surface.

Fly line, sink-tip: A fly line that has a weighted portion at the tip to take and keep the fly underwater, the weighted portion being of varying lengths and densities, to affect the depth to which the fly sinks and the speed with which it sinks. (See sink rate.)

Fly line, weight-forward: A fly line with a taper, in which the heaviest portion is toward the end to which the tippet and fly are attached.

Fry: The fish just after it has hatched from the egg.

Gape: the distance between the hook shank and the point; it determines hook size. Also called gap.

Graphite: Material used in the manufacture of strong, flexible, and lightweight fly rods.

Grayling, Arctic: A member of the salmonid family generally found in only pure, cold water and characterized by its huge, sail-like dorsal fin.

Guide: The metal or ceramic loops set along a fly rod through which the line passes. Also, one who assists another to fish.

Hackle: Feathers from a chicken or game bird's neck or back that are used in making artificial flies.

Handle: The cork grip of a rod the angler holds when casting. Also, the piece of metal that turns the spool on a fly reel.

Hatch: The time when large numbers of insects emerge from the surface of the water or nearby vegetation and become airborne.

Haul: A swift, short pull on the fly line during the cast to achieve more distance; called a "double haul" when done on both the front cast and backcast.

Hip boots: Waterproof protection for wading, covering the legs only; may be made of rubber, neoprene, or breathable materials and may include attached boots or be worn with separate boots. (See waders.)

Hit: When a fish bites an artificial fly.

Hold: A spot in a river or stream where fish can rest or wait for the current to deliver food; often located behind an obstruction, such as a submerged rock, or along undercut banks with slow, deep current. (See feeding lie.)

Hook eye: The small ring or loop at the front of the hook to which the leader is attached.

Hook shank: The long part of the hook between the hook eye and the bend.

Hook size: A number determined by the width of the hook gape (not the length of the shank). The larger the number, the smaller the hook, i.e. size 24 is a very small hook, while size 4 is a large hook.

Knot. blood: A knot used to tie segments of monofilament line of different diameter together to construct a leader or attach a tippet to a leader.

Knot, improved clinch: A knot used most frequently to tie a fly to a leader.

Knot, nail: A knot used to connect a loop of heavy monofilament to the fly line, in order to attach a leader using the loop-to-loop connection.

Knot. surgeon's: A knot used to tie segments of monofilament line of different diameter together to construct a leader or attach a tippet to a leader.

Landing: Bringing a fish to the angler or the boat.

Larva: One of the underwater life stages of aquatic insects, such as caddisflies.

Leader: The length of nylon monofilament that extends from the fly line to the fly. It can be a knotless leader made from a single, tapered strand of nylon or one in which several pieces of monofilament of decreasing diameter are connected by blood or surgeon's knots.

Leech: An aquatic worm found in streams and lakes; often referred to as a bloodsucker. A favorite food of fish. Also, a fly that imitates a leech.

Line hand: The hand that holds the fly line while casting and fishing. (See rod hand.)

Line weight: a measure of a fly line related to the size and strength of rod that should be used to cast it, based on the actual weight of the first thirty feet of the line.

Load/loading: When the weight of the fly line bends the rod tip during casting.

Mayfly: An aquatic insect that is a favorite food of fish. Adults have upswept wings and tails.

Mending: Using the rod tip to move the fly line and leader into a different position, either in the air or on the water, to enable the fly to float without drag. Usually achieved with an upstream flip of the rod tip.

Milt: The male fish's reproductive secretions.

Monofilament: Single-strand nylon fishing line used in fly fishing for leaders.

Nippers: Clippers or similar cutting tools used to trim the tag ends of knots.

Nymph: One of the underwater life stages of aquatic insects, such as mayflies. Also, the type of artificial fly that imitates any of the underwater life stages of insects.

Palming: Pressing the palm of the line hand against the exposed outer rim of a fly reel in order to slow the run of a hooked fish.

Pickup: Lifting the fly line off the water with a fly rod in the first stage of the cast.

Play: The act of controlling and fighting a fish that is hooked.

Polarization: Treatment in the manufacture of sunglasses that reduces glare to enable the angler to see the fish under the surface of the water.

Pool: A slow-moving part of a river, usually with significant depth, the surface of which is usually unbroken.

Pound test: The breaking strength of nylon monofilament fishing line. Presentation: Placement of the fly on the water. Also, the way the fly is fished. Pupa: One of the underwater life stages of aquatic insects, such as caddisflies.

Rapids: Where the water of a river flows with great force over and around large boulders.

Redd: The nest in the sand or gravel of a river that a female fish creates with her body or her tail and into which she drops her eggs.

Reel foot: The fitting at the bottom of a fly reel that attaches to the reel seat.

Reel seat: The area near the bottom of a fly rod, below the handle, where the reel is placed and secured by a locking device.

Riffles: Where the water of a river flows over small stones or rocks and causes lots of bubbles or foam, typically in shallow water.

Rise: When a fish comes to the surface of the water to eat an insect or an artificial fly.

Rod hand: The hand that holds the fly rod while casting and fishing. (See line hand.)

Rod weight: A term in casual usage to indicate the line weight a rod is designed to cast, as in a four-weight rod.

Roe: Fish eggs.

Run: A section of water in a river that typically flows more slowly and deeply than the water either directly upstream or downstream. Also, the action of a fish that is hooked and being played by the angler.

Salmonid: Any of a family of elongate, soft-finned fishes (such as salmon and trout) that have the last vertebrae upturned.

Sink rate: How fast the tip of a sink-tip fly line sinks in the water.

Slack: Line that is loose and without tension. Some slack line facilitates a drag-free drift of the fly, but too much enables the fish to shake the hook loose.

Smolt: Juvenile salmon or trout as it migrates to the sea for the first time; a major food source for larger fish.

Spawn: The reproductive activity of fish, in which the female digs a redd and lays eggs while the male swims alongside and releases milt to fertilize them.

Split-shot: Small balls of lead or lead substitute of different sizes, which an angler can pinch onto the leader to make the leader and fly sink.

Streamer: An artificial fly that imitates bait fish or leeches.

Strike: When a fish bites an artificial fly.

Strike indicator: A material attached to the leader or end of the fly line to help the angler tell when a fish has taken an underwater fly, such as a nymph; usually a small piece of floating, colored foam or cork, but also a plastic bead or a small puff of yarn.

Stripping: Pulling in the fly line with the line hand while the line is held by the fingers of the rod hand; done to take in slack, play a fish, or add movement to the fly.

Stripping guide: A metal or ceramic loop on the fly rod closest to the handle.

Stonefly: An aquatic insect that lives mainly in streams among the rocks and migrates to shore to metamorphose into an adult; in both nymph and adult stages, a significant food source for fish.

Tailing: Landing a fish by grasping it just in front of its tail. Also, a particular kind of subsurface feeding activity by fish during which their tails show above the water.

Tailing loop: A loop in a fly line during casting, caused by the fly line dropping below the tip of the rod during an improperly executed cast; usually results in the fly not being delivered correctly.

Take: When a fish bites an artificial fly.

Tide: The periodic rise and fall of oceans and other waters as a result of the moon's gravitational pull.

Tippet: The portion of the leader to which the fly is tied.

Troll: To tow a fly or lure behind a moving boat or float tube.

Upstream: The direction from which river water flows toward the angler.

Waders: Chest-high, waterproof protection worn over an angler's clothes and covering the legs and chest; may be made of rubber, neoprene, or breathable materials and may include attached boots or be worn with separate boots. (See hip boots.)

Wading stick/staff: A stick or staff used by a fly fisher to help provide stability while wading in rivers or streams; usually metal, collapsible, and carried in a belt pouch.

Wet fly: An artificial fly fished under the water and used to imitate insects, leeches, small fish, and crustaceans.

Wind knot: A knot that forms in the leader and is caused by incorrect casting techniques or, occasionally, by the wind.

APPENDIX 3
FLY FISHING OPPORTUNITIES FOR YOUNG PEOPLE

FIRST CAST, TROUT UNLIMITED
Go online to www.tu.org/site/pp.asp?c=7dJEKTNuFmG&b=404569 for more information or search for "first cast trout unlimited."

THE ANNUAL FFF FLY FISHING YOUTH CAMP
IN LIVINGSTON, MONTANA
Go online to www.fedflyfishers.org/edForKidsProgramDetails.php for more information or search for "fff for kids program."

TROUT/SALMON IN THE CLASSROOM
Contact your state or local Department of Fish and Game, Fish and Wildlife, or similar government agency for more information.

GIRL SCOUTS OF AMERICA
An organization founded to help girls build character and gain skills for success in the real world. Their web site can help you find a regional council and a local troop in which to participate. Many troops offer fly fishing as one of their outdoor activities. See www.girlscouts.org/.

GIRL GUIDES OF CANADA
Headquartered in Toronto, GGC is an organization for girls and women that offers a variety of activities, including fly fishing. Visit their web site at www.girlguides.ca/default.asp?id=80 for more information.

APPENDIX 4
FLYFISHING CLUBS FOR WOMMEN

UNITED STATES OF AMERICA

Arizona
Dame Juliana Anglers
1332 E. Redfield Rd. Tempe, AZ 85283
Web site: www.devpros.com/dja

Delaware/Pennsylvania
Delaware Valley Women's Fly Fishing
Association
25 Marple Rd.
Haverford, PA 19041
Web site: www.dvwffa.org

California
Golden West Women Fly Fishers
790 27th Ave.
San Francisco, CA 94121
Web site: www.gwwf.org

The Ladybugs Fly Fishers Club
3340 Lariat Dr.
Cameron Park, CA 95682
Web site: www.theladybugs.com

Shasta Mayflies
2384 Hawn Ave.
Redding, CA 96002

Colorado
Colorado Women Flyfishers
P.O. Box 101137
Denver, CO 80250-1137
Web site: www.colowomenflyfishers.org

Connecticut
Connecticut Women Anglers on the Fly
24 Dryden Dr.
Meriden, CT 06450

Florida
The Bonefish Bonnies Ocean Reef Club
32 Cardinal Lane
Key Largo, FL 33037

Georgia
Georgia Women Flyfishers
828 Burton Ridge Drive
Loganville, GA 30052
Web site: www.georgiaflyfishing.com

Illinois
Chicago Women's Casting & Angling
Club 1400 N. State Parkway, Suite #8-A
Chicago, IL 60610

Maine
Tacky Women's Angler Team
P.O. Box 1
Anson, ME 04911

Maryland/Virginia
Chesapeake Women Anglers
P.O. Box 19156 Alexandria, VA 22320
Web site:
www.chesa pea kewomena nglers.org

Michigan
Flygirls of Michigan, Inc.
c/o J. Nelson
7315 S. Altadena Royal Oak, Ml 48067
Web site: www.flygirls.ws

Minnesota
Women Anglers of Minnesota
P.O. Box 580653 Minneapolis, MN 55468
Web site: www.up-north.com/
womenanglers/

Montana
Gallatin Valley Wad'n Women
13840 Kelly Canyon Rd.
Bozeman, MT 59715-8203

New Jersey
Joan Wulff Fly Fishers
Box 1782
Passaic, NJ 07055

New York
Dame Anglers 5 Lower Rd.
Westtown, NY 10998

Juliana's Anglers
FDR Station;
P.O. Box 7220 New York, NY 10150

North Carolina
Women On The Fly
4732 Sharon Rd.
Charlotte, NC 28210

Stonefly Maidens
P.O. Box 82412
Portland, OR 97282-0412
Web site: www.stoneflymaidens.org

Rhode Island
Ladies of the Long Rod 203 Sterling Ave.
Providence, RI 02909

South Carolina
Women In Waders
109 Country Club Ct.
Spartanbury, SC 29302

Texas
Texas Women Fly Fishers 7310 S.
Congress, #106
Austin, TX 78745
Web site: www.twff.net

Virginia
Reelladies
2756 Avenal Ave. SW
Roanoke, VA 24015

The Lady Highlanders
16501 Jeb Stuart Highway (Rt. 58)
Abingdon, VA 24211

Washington
Northwest Women Flyfishers
P.O. Box 31020
Seattle, WA 98103-1020
Web site: www.northwestwomenfly
fishers.com

Oregon
Damsel Flies Box 3932
Eugene, OR 97402

Southwest Washington Lady Flyfishers
110 Penny Lane
Kelso, WA 98626

FOREIGN COUNTRIES

Canada
Ottawa Women Fly Fishers
2659 Ayers Ave.
Ottawa, ON K1V 7W7 Canada

Reel Women Fly fishing Club
2039 Chrisdon Rd.
Burlington, ON L7M 3W8 Canada

Ireland
Irish Ladies Fly Fishing Association
Web site:
irishladiesflyfish ing.com/about0/o20us/
aboutus_home.html

Japan
Japan Fly Fishers Women
C/0 Japan Fly Fishers
Bl Kodama Bldg, 1-1-1
Chuo Nakano-ku, Tokyo, 164-0011 Japan

New Zealand
Tauranga Anglers Club Incorporated
PO Box 14018
Tauranga, North Island New Zealand

United Kingdom
England Ladies Fly Fisher Association
2 Dukes Place
Herringthrope Rotherham S65 3BG
Great Britain
Web site: www.elfa.org.uk/

Wales
Welsh Ladies Angling Division (WLAD)
Spring Gardens
Parrog Rd. Newport Pembs 420RJ
West Wales, SA Great Britain

Note: Addresses and other contact
information for these clubs will change
over time. Please visit their web sites or
www.womenfiyfishing.net for the most
current information.

FLYFISHING BOOKS BY WOMEN

Cast Again: Tales of a Fly-Fishing Guide, Jennifer Olsson, 1997, The Lyons Press, New York.

Cathy Beck's Fly-Fishing Handbook, Cathy Beck, 1996, The Lyons Press, New York.

A Different Angle: Fly Fishing Stories by Women, Holly Morris, editor, 1995, Seal Press, Seattle, WA.

Fly Fishing: A Woman's Guide, Dana Rikimaru, 2000, Ragged Mountain Press/ McGraw-Hill, Camden, ME.

Fly Fishing Women Explore Alaska, Cecilia "Pudge" Kleinkauf, 2003, Epicenter Press, Kenmore, WA.

Joan Wulff's Fly-Casting Accuracy, Joan Wulff, 1997, The Lyons Press, New York.

Joan Wulff's Fly-Casting Techniques, Joan Wulff, 1995, The Lyons Press, New York.

Joan Wulff's Fly Fishing: Expert Advice From a Woman's Perspective, Joan Wulff, 1991, Stackpole Books, Mechanicsburg, PA.

Little Rivers: Tales of a Woman Angler, Margot Page, 1995, The Lyons Press, New York.

On The Mother Lagoon: Fly Fishing and the Spiritual Journey, Kathy Sparrow, 2003, Wish Publishing, Terre Haute, IN.

Positive Fly Fishing, Marla Blair, 2005, The Lyons Press, New York.

Reel Women: The World of Women Who Fish, Lyla Foggia, 1995, Beyond Words Publishing, Hillsboro, OR.

Reading the Water: Stories and Essays of Fly fishing and Life, Mallory Burton and Holly Morris, 1995, Keokee Company Publishing, Sandpoint, ID.

A Woman's Guide To Fly Fishing Favorite Waters, Yvonne Graham, editor, 2000, David Communications, Sisters, Oregon.

PHOTO CREDITS

The creative eye and technical expertise of professional photographer Michael DeYoung are evident in his photographs of river girls Alyssa and Samantha. Those of Samantha were taken over a span of several years.

His contributions to this book depict the beauty of fly fishing and the intensity with which the girls pursue it.

His photographs of the river girls appear on i, ii-iii, iv, vi, xiv, 4, 6-7, 16, 18, 20, 22, 30-32, 34, 40-42, 47-48, 51-52, 55-57, 59-60, 62-63, 66, 71-74, 76-77, 79, 81, 84, 92, 94-96, 98, 100-104, 108-110, 112, 114, 116-120, 123-126, 128, 130, 132-134, 136, 142.

Michael's outstanding photographs of Alaska are available for viewing and purchase at www.mdphoto.com.

The following photographers also contributed to the book: Donna O'Sullivan appears on viii, Mattias P. Rosell on 8 and Chris Korich on 138.

Christy Ruby, the illustrator of River Girls, is an Alaska native artist. In addition to her illustrations, Christy provided the photographs of insects and freshwater flies found in Chapter 9.

Christy's artistry can be seen at www.acsalaska.net/~crdesign/.

Cabela's, a major retailer in fishing and hunting gear and clothing, provided the photographs of waders in Chapter 11. Their online store is located at www.cabelas.com.

AUTHOR CECILIA "PUDGE" KLEINKAUF

Pudge Kleinkauf has owned and operated her instruction and guide service, Women's Fly fishing, for nineteen of the thirty-six years she has lived and fished in Alaska. During that time, Pudge has introduced countless women to the joys of fly fishing in locations all around the 49th State and in Mexico.

Pudge is also a contributor to *A Woman's No Nonsense Guide To Fly Fishing Favorite Waters*, edited by Yvonne Graham. Her articles have appeared in Northwest Fly Fishing, Fly Fish America, The Island Fish Finder, the Journal of the International Grayling Society, and Fish Alaska Magazine, where she is also a contributing editor. She is the author of Fly Fishing Women Explore Alaska. She also serves as a volunteer instructor for Alaska's Casting for Recovery retreat for breast cancer survivors, for girl scout camps in Alaska, and for the Alaska Department of Fish and Game's Salmon in the Classroom program.

Since 1995, Pudge's company, Women's Fly fishing, has maintained the internet's leading web site for women who fly fish (www.womensflyfishing.net). With the publication of River Girls, Pudge has introduced a web site (www.rivergirlsflyfishing.com) where girls can post photos and stories of the fish, they catch on a fly rod.

PHOTOGRAPER MICHAEL DEYOUNG

Michael DeYoung is a longtime Alaskan well known for his stunning images of the outdoors. A trained meteorologist, as well as a professional photographer, his understanding of weather and light unquestionably enhances his photographic talents.

Mike does not simply capture nature in a unique way. His special artistry is showing people savoring their favorite outdoor sport. An avid fly fisher himself, his images of young women fly fishing illustrate River Girls.

Mike's photos have appeared in numerous magazines and print ads around the country. His photography illustrates Pudge Kleinkaufs first book, Fly Fishing Women Explore Alaska. His work has appeared in Alaska Magazine, Adventure West, National Geographic, New Age Journal, and many other publications. He is also a regular contributor to the annual Alaska Milepost. His web site (www.mdphoto.com) contains examples of his work.

ILLUSTRATOR CHRISTY RUBY

Christy Ruby is a lifelong Alaska native fly fisher and fly-tier, wetting a line whenever and wherever she can. Her hand-tied polar bear flies are sold throughout Alaska.

Besides being a skilled illustrator of books and magazine articles, she has designed wall murals and sculpted over 200 coins for private mints around the United States.

Christy's artistry can be seen online at www.acsalaska.net/~crdesign/.

CPSIA information can be obtained
at www.ICGtesting.com
Printed in the USA
BVHW021231140719
553410BV00004B/8/P